A JOURNEY TO AFGHANISTAN

TRAVELS IN AN AWAKENING COUNTRY

ROGER WILLEMSEN

JAICO PUBLISHING HOUSE

Ahmedabad Bangalore Bhopal Bhubaneswar Chennai
Delhi Hyderabad Kolkata Lucknow Mumbai

Published by Jaico Publishing House
A-2 Jash Chambers, 7-A Sir Phirozshah Mehta Road
Fort, Mumbai - 400 001
jaicopub@jaicobooks.com
www.jaicobooks.com

Published in arrangement with
Haus Publishing
26 Cadogan Court, Draycott Avenue
London SW3 3BX

A JOURNEY TO AFGHANISTAN
ISBN 978-81-8495-254-4

First Jaico Impression: 2011
Reissued: 2013
Originally published as *An Afghan Journey*

Printed by
Kaveri Printers Pvt. Ltd.
19, Ansari Road, Darya Ganj
New Delhi - 110 002

1

In the dark I hear the gardener sweeping the veranda with a besom broom. A little later a dustcart stops, and from the neighbouring room comes the scraping sound of a window shutter being opened. The dirty light that pours through the half-open shutter is mixed with mist. It is a moist light.

That was on the morning of the last Saturday in October 2005. I was to appear at an event that evening in Locarno, but had arrived the day before to prepare for my journey to Afghanistan in the legendary Grand Hotel – three days before it was to close, perhaps forever. The days were so sunny that you could sit outside in a light jacket. The hotel lay there, dark and immense. Its long corridors, its lounges and drawing rooms were already resigned to their end, dusty and seemingly covered with a layer of varnish.

In the stairwell hung the biggest candelabra in the world, made of Murano glass, like coloured crystals of sugar. Its buds shot out like tumours. Darkly patinated seascapes and engravings on the walls, solid 19th-century furniture on the faded carpets with their sun-bleached edges, and on the ceiling frescos in the lounges naked female athletes, with wings. A pale-skinned Europa being taken on a bull to a heaven already glimmering with verdigris, up into the great wilting and dying that has also brought cracks and moss to the balconies outside.

I'd spread the travel books out on the table, Robert Byron, Bruce Chatwin, Peter Levi, Nicolas Bouvier, Doris Lessing, William T. Vollmann, Saira Shah and others – as well as books of photographs, a street map, a map of the countryside, and the snaps that my Afghan friend Nadia had lent me: her sisters in a Kunduz garden or playing volleyball, people who smilingly greet the spring in their traditional clothing, pictures from the country's happier years.

The manager opened the terrace on the first floor just one more time, so that I could drink a last cup of coffee there. Not all the shutters were still intact, not all the windows could still close, and the food in the pantry might well have outlasted the hotel.

This is where a journey starts into a country that has only been open for a few weeks, decades after having been written off as a ruin.

Every journey begins with memories, in the fog that surrounds a name. 'Afghanistan' – surrounded by smoke and dust, encircled by images in sandstone and lapis lazuli, by theatrical mountains and steppes, by the landscapes of faces that could belong to apostles.

I can still see the frenzied little horse riders in the Indian miniatures that as a child illustrated the foreign for me, where furious Mongols and Turkmen competed against athletic Afghans in equestrian games. Women with graceful necks, and eyes accentuated by curving black lines, held out their hands to courtiers. Falconers could be seen, along with gardeners tending bitter orange trees, and Afghan nobles, 'rugged, proud and independent', with 'their turbans on their shaven heads', as it said.

And then there was the Hippy Trail that a good 100,000 young Westerners went on, fed by green and black Afghan hash, later to return with matted hair, smoking the 'weed of the poor' and stammering something about 'indescribable'. I can still see 'my' homecomer, how he wandered lost around his parents' flat repeating the same phrase: 'So that's how you live, so that's how you live.' Nothing stood firm.

The room in the Grand Hotel is enormous, but furnished with two camp beds. I spread out the newer books on them. Almost all have women in the burka on their covers – obviously Afghanistan is only recognizable by pleated veils covering the whole body, ruined tanks and horseback sports. Emphasizing the foreign like this puts obstacles on our path to identifying with it.

I read about hippies, the Taliban and warlords, about Pashtuns, Tajiks, Uzbeks and Turkmen nomads. Names like 'Salang Pass' and 'Panjshir Valley' crop up. Past travellers headed for the legendary border river in the north, the Oxus, while contemporaries visited Bamyan where the statues of the Buddha had been blown up. A spicy mix of names.

Others recapitulate Britain's, Russia's, America's, even Pakistan's and Iran's foreign policy towards Afghanistan, in actual fact a military policy. For out of ignorance or a lack of scruples, the world's political players built this land, an area home to many peoples, into a strategic power. At the same time literary travellers look back dreamily to a past that is spoken about as if it were a lost paradise.

In 1981 Bruce Chatwin could look back and write: 'In 1962 – six years before the Hippies wrecked it (by driving educated Afghans into the arms of the Marxists) – you could set off to Afghanistan with the anticipations of, say, Delacroix off to Algiers. On the streets of Herat you saw men in mountainous turbans, strolling hand in hand, with roses in their mouths and rifles wrapped in flowered chintz. In Badakhshan you could picnic on Chinese carpets and listen to the bulbul.'

The political strategists and the literary travellers didn't surrender to the same country. Nor did it surrender to them: they failed – militarily due to the country's guerrilla mentality, aesthetically due to its erratic nature. Those involved know it. Military and literary statements about not matching up to Afghanistan seem related. Capitulation left, right and centre.

The country embodied itself for me most happily in Nadia, who I met 15 years ago at a documentary film festival: tall, her eyebrows and lashes painted black, her hair thick, she stood there, wrapped in colourful fabrics and – most of all – in her charisma and her past: she was a revelation. You could see how her presence made people feel unsure – how to talk to someone like that?

2

Every journey that you describe begins with the question 'Where was I?' In both senses. Where was the thread of the story interrupted, and how do you find out where you really were?

It begins with an exploration of this one unmistakable land and ends with the general question of how people become attached to places they had gone to in search of the foreign. The painter Odilon Redon in his notes *To Myself* enthused about a time when people would only enter 'another land out of admiration or sympathy'. Afghanistan hasn't had many such visitors in the past 30 years; instead four million exiles have carried Afghanistan into the world like a blue flower. In their homesickness the country is present everywhere.

'Once upon a time there was – or was there?' So begin Afghan fairy tales. Once upon a time there was the legendary city of Kabul where a bohemian life took root in which women wore miniskirts, and an ancient culture let in a young one – Afghanistan and anarchy.

'When the traveller arriving from the south catches sight of Kabul,' writes Nicolas Bouvier, 'its girdle of poplars, its mauve mountains on which a thin layer of snow steams, and the kites fluttering in the autumn sky above the bazaar, he prides himself on having arrived at the world's end. He has in fact reached its centre.' Or has he? Images surrounded by more images.

I was still in Locarno.

~

The taxi driver gets lost on the way to the airport. 'I'm not really your hotel and airport type. I specialize in disabled people and grannies.'

The sun is setting red.

'That's beautiful!' escapes my lips.

'Yes,' the driver replies. 'Thank you.' He says it as if the sun were part of his taxi's interior fittings.

'... And your airline? From Dubai with Ariana – the never-come-back line?' The question slips out of the German check-in woman's mouth. '*I* wouldn't fly with them.'

It looks as though even the air routes to Kabul are dirt tracks.

~

Where are you travelling? Into sight. Where do you want to arrive? In clear view. What do you see, what pushes you on? The image of a head resting on an arm. The image of a slender, workworn hand that passes the tea, laughter underlaid with the honking of car horns, air-conditioning blowing cold, rum-tipsy times, long painted fingernails. A bargain bin of stereotypes. Where are you travelling? From a state of waiting to the end of all interim conditions, to where headlines and slogans have fallen silent, to where you can move on your own, towards a borrowed loss of your self, a different feeling for time.

In the scattered light of the departure lounge for flights from Frankfurt to the Arab world you see politicizing North Africans, old women carrying whole cultural spaces with them, those returning home with bursting Aldi bags, exiles with scarce goods, pruning shears or a bird cage; among them all a girl on crutches who has just had an operation, and German policemen and trainers, mourners too, accompanying a coffin home. Weaving between them are shady looking Europeanized Afghans and Persians who introduce themselves as 'mediators', with their names in silver on business cards. 'In case you need my services …' they whisper. 'In Kabul take a Pashtun as your interpreter. All the others are liars or work for the secret service.'

The queue nudges forwards, towards 'Attraction', an advert for 'The New Fragrance for Women', on the other side of which is a Wanted poster for Arab terrorists. Some of them have already been crossed out with a red felt pen.

Then we've left the country.

Where will we arrive? I try to remember.

Nadia is wearing a red gauze veil that she has wrapped around her head, alluding to the coming country. She looks magnificent in the opulence of her festive colours. Her make-up, too, is Afghan now – she has a wide black line on her eyelids and I already feel awkward for wanting to greet her with a hug. After all, fully veiled women are sitting there, probably wives from the United Arab Emirates, shopping victims in nuns' habits. But Christian, the photographer, gives her the same greeting and Nadia is cheerful and at ease. Still time for a coffee, accompanied by some truffles sprinkled with sugar, which she offers us in a red heart-shaped box.

~

We are travelling to a country that has just had elections on the same day as Germany, and they resulted in a chaos no greater than that in Germany. The final count is not yet in, but is expected any day. In Germany the head of the Social Democrats, Franz Müntefering, resigns with the stoic face of a Christmas nutcracker figure. Wherever you look there are lobbyists, pressure groups, representatives and spokespeople, all busy stamping the interests of their tribe with the seal 'Germany'. It's always for the good of 'our country'.

What about a campaign with the slogan 'You are Afghanistan'? No one would dream of it. You illiterate, you widower, you cripple, you murderer, you fighter, you drug grower, you burka-wearing beggar, you madman, you exile, you jailbird, you tramp, you street child, all you wretched people, you shouldn't be Afghanistan, but you are. But who would want to define a country's so-called identity by those who have failed in it?

A post-war country lies ahead of us, full of terrible inner and outer devastation. It could just as well be a pre-war country. We'll travel past knocked-out tanks from the last 25 years to the ruins left by the latest US bombing raids, into a mined capital, into a country of hostage taking and sniping.

I'm not there yet, but after talking in the airport and on the Ariana jet to German soldiers and businessmen, and to Afghan officials and exiles, my first impression is that all have the same Germany, but different Afghanistans.

Amanda Peet smiles a wide Southern belle smile from the in-flight film. It's just a conventional comedy with its light moments, but it's not the content that etches itself into my mind. I can now see the country below me in Cinemascope while in front of me a naked Amanda Peet shimmers near a night-time wooded lake. She snaps her boyfriend with a camera that she holds in front of her breasts, the subtitles cover her stomach. They can't be more free. This way of dealing with nakedness: Hollywood's burka.

In the transit airport at Dubai at two in the morning the waiting passengers squeeze themselves into the moulded seats designed to prevent people from lying down. Exhausted, they wrap themselves in blankets on the floor, between displays of saffron sugar needles and rows of dog shampoos, as if to keep alive the idea of a holding room for people, the idea of a camp, while they wait until six in the morning for the flight to Kabul. Outside the camp are holidaymakers all with the same sports bags, Asian women in tête-à-têtes, extreme shoppers, tattooed builders, Bangladeshi pilgrims, heavily laden Africans, mobile phone users of all tongues, and homecomers in their Tchibo cyclists' jerseys.

And then this young veiled woman from Germany was there, the only Afghan among all the worker bees from Saudi Arabia. But she appeared so vulnerable and nervous that Nadia notices her, and helps her, because she doesn't yet have a boarding pass.

Salema, that's her name, is trying to look like a seasoned traveller, but her face seems churned up and restless below the surface. Nadia recognizes from her speech that she's a second generation exile who's probably never seen her homeland. Even her voice sounds nervous, not least because her luggage is travelling separately. There are, of course, receipts and torn-off dockets to be shown at the baggage desk. Employees in white coats are clambering about between suitcases and bags, like hospital orderlies looking for their lost patients.

We are shuttled out in a shabby minibus. Salema has been to the duty-free and now has a bag labelled Gold Luxury. The bus stops to let off some uniformed ground staff. Barely out of the bus, they all lean their heads backwards to breathe in the warm night air.

On the aeroplane I'm still constantly confronted by choices: coffee with or without, champagne with or without, mineral water with or without, which dressing on my salad, cheesecake with or without passion fruit syrup. I'm going to a country without choices. Next to me a man is seriously nonplussed because they don't have *slightly* sparkling mineral water.

Then the memory of an injured Afghan patient who was flown to the West to be operated on. From his hospital room the convalescent saw a woman in her underwear cleaning a window. He exclaimed, 'You live shamelessly! Your lives are pornographic!' What can we say to that?

The flight attendant comes with the dessert trolley. 'Good thing you've left some space, it's worth it,' he says.

The unconscious obscenity of wealth: in the midst of excess to leave room for more excess, and as soon as you no longer feel full, you think you're hungry.

The man sitting next to me tells me of the first blow landed by Afghan workers in their struggle: the cobblers in Kabul are demonstrating against the Chinese, whose cheap imports are ruining their trade in beautifully crafted shoes. With peace has come globalization, the marketplace has become a battleground.

~

Deserts run into snow-covered mountains, the light yellow of the sand leads into a dazzling white, an evacuated landscape. The Hindu Kush with its closely pleated mountain ranges and its karakul patterning: it lies there like a spring flood made of stone, with heavy rolling waves of rock.

'Kabul for the most part has an easy unpretentious character, as of a Balkan town in the good sense of the term', wrote Robert Byron in 1933. 'Snow-mountains decorate the distance, the parliament sits in a cornfield, and long avenues shade the town's approaches. [...] Cinemas and alcohol are forbidden. The Legation doctor has had to give up treating women at the instance of the Church; though they sometimes visit him disguised as boys. And the whole policy of forcible westernization is in abeyance. All the same, westernization is progressing by example, and one feels that perhaps the Afghans have struck the mean for which Asia is looking.'

Early travellers spoke of the merciless heat, the impassable roads and the dangerous animals, marshes, fevers and epidemics. In the mountains they faced it all with stiff doses of whisky and snow. From the aeroplane, at first you see spiky gables of rock above the compressed bulk of mountains, a frozen movement, nothing more. Then the ice deserts turn to deserts of sand. In this landscape human beings look like a lost species.

A German journalist spoke in favour of the US bombing of Afghanistan in autumn 2001, saying that 'the civilian population of Afghanistan', let's be honest, 'doesn't matter at all to us'. That makes it different to the civilian populations of Dresden, New York or Tel Aviv, and has made it easier for some people to agree to hunting terrorists using carpet bombing that they themselves aren't affected by. Strange that in approving of mass deaths – breaking a taboo – people see themselves as daring, while simply focusing on individual suffering seems anachronistic.

It's just that to cynics Afghanistan is a victim state. In the past decades few countries have fallen as hard as Afghanistan has. The country appears before us as a mass of suffering and not as King Amanullah once saw it, as 'Asia's Switzerland'.

Nadia's world is this Afghanistan of the liberal Sixties and Seventies. Her father owned a cinema, a theatre, a museum and a library in Kunduz. Today only the first of these is still standing, reminding everyone of the dreams they went there to see. For a time the theatre provided shelter and accommodation, and was also a symbol of decadence. Into the Seventies Czech mime artists, Russian opera and ballet, and Turkish, Indian and Afghan theatre and dance could be seen there. Neither the theatre or the cinema became subversive through their own actions, the changes around them made them subversive. The same was happening throughout the country.

I'm reading Doris Lessing's 1987 book on Afghanistan, *The Wind Blows Away Our Words*. For the German translation, which was published in 2002, she wrote a new foreword. In it she relies on the second-hand facts of newspaper reporting for her realist politics. 'The war in Afghanistan,' she writes, 'will enable (we hope) strategic targets to be bombed with precision. It can end the Taliban rule.'

She goes on to demand 'modesty of ambition', 'some good old-fashioned common sense' and 'a little scepticism'. The new foreword ends with a postscript: 'We have just heard that the first bombs have fallen on Afghanistan.'

Maybe Doris Lessing is an exemplary case. She worked for an NGO in Afghanistan for many years and yet after September 11th she fell into using the warmongers' rhetoric.

Until then she most probably knew that 'strategic targets' are just as illusory as 'precision' bombing and that the phrases' formality is in stark contrast to the actual reality. She certainly also understood that appeals to common sense, realism and caution only mean one thing in times of war: they allow the speakers to appear moderate and humane. Yet no one is, who speaks in favour of 'precision' bombing.

~

The descent towards Kabul – structures scratched into the dirt, all of the same shade, the outlines of the settlements like crystalline natural forms, the squares of the blocks of houses intact, rolled out like miles of deep carpet. Surrounding walls, walls standing on their own, bomb craters, areas grazed raw. The earth's skin beaten to a pulp, damaged and scabbed.

~

Kabul Airport has been built to appear more than it is. Inside there are dark corridors, makeshift counters, walls peeling to reveal wiring and pipes, and a panting conveyor belt that spits luggage out of a hole in the wall into the extremely overcrowded hall.

Among those waiting for their luggage are heavily cloaked women, yes, but they are wearing colourful rings and bracelets, and have jewels, elaborate patterns and braid trimming woven into their burkas. On the one hand there is an attempt to create individuality and breathe life into the basic kit, on the other hand new markets stake claims to women's bodies, even veiled ones. I buy a sachet of Titanic Shampoo, on which Kate Winslet's face has been drawn in colour.

'Did you,' I ask the homecoming bus driver who is waiting at the baggage carrousel with me, 'find a candidate you could trust among those in the elections?'

'No,' he smiles resignedly, already as weary of democracy as any old man from the West. 'But it could have been so good.'

Just then a nearby American grabs a tool case. His T-shirt is emblazoned with the words 'Tear Down Team'.

~

We're still standing under a flickering neon light in this room of unplastered breeze blocks that stands in for an airport hall. It hasn't accommodated all the passengers yet and it's already too full. Airport staff pick their way over suitcases and packages. Individual, hotly disputed items are still issuing from the hole in the wall. Some are greeted like people.

In the midst of it all is Nadia, friendly and helpful, ready for anything, indeed embracing it all – from the confusion at the conveyor belt to the men's scuffling over her possessions, the baggage handlers' orders and the demands of the inspectors for baggage counterfoils. The faces in the room are a hundred years old. Worn hands carry packages in bubble wrap and cellophane, as well as homemade suitcases and bundles of things tied together. We can see a crowd squatting and waiting outside, dusty light, a swept front square, ruins on both sides.

3

Salema can't really believe that her blue suitcase will have made the journey from the Saarland to Kabul at the same time as her. Her story reveals itself almost *en passant*. When she was eight the mujaheddin killed her parents. An Afghan orphan, her aunts soon sent her to distant relatives in Germany.

This really is her first visit back to Afghanistan. She's expecting her aunt, but isn't sure that her aunt will recognize her. Nor does she know what's in store for her, what expectations will accompany her visit and whether she's prepared for the coming weeks in the Afghan town of Ghazni. She's taken care to put on black clothes and spread a veil over her hair, but who knows what details are Western without her knowing it? Dressing appropriately, avoiding men, that can all be learnt, but what about the way she walks, her gestures, the strength of her voice, her character?

Ghazni, once a Taliban stronghold, is today a town in ruins. It will demand a lot of Salema. Then, miraculously, her suitcase arrives. She doesn't want to go yet though, not before we've got our own luggage.

'Can you tell the Tajiks and Pashtuns apart?'

She nods.

‘So, which people do you actually belong to?’

She traces the outline of her face with her pointed fingers. ‘This eastern shape, see, the almond shape,’ she says pointing to her eyes, cheekbones and the contours of her skull as if they all formed a single almond, ‘is Tajik. I’m a Tajik.’

Nadia adds that because of their nomadic origins you can still recognize the Pashtuns and other mountain peoples by their lengthy stride, their expansive gestures and the loud voices with which they’ve always made themselves heard over the wind, the distances and their noisy herds.

On the square I shake Salema’s hand in parting, some distance from the cordoned-off people waiting for homecomers. This public handshake between a man and a woman is, even though we come from the West, almost too much. When Nadia hugs Salema I see her lips quiver.

But when she lets go of Nadia, a rippling group of worried little women hurries over as if electrified. They do recognize each other. The aunt, her spitting image, is wearing a blue cloak and barely needs to look in Salema’s eyes. She just takes her head in both her hands and kisses her forehead again and again, then she lavishes a diagonal line of kisses over her face. There are no tears, but the aunt keeps wiping her nose.

A few auxiliary figures stand around observing solemnly. Then the little pack starts moving, the aunt in her dusty blue garment, Salema with her blue suitcase – colour sisters. They finally get into a tiny car and set off for the south. Does the aunt know that Salema won’t stay forever, that she wants to return from the countryside to Kabul, and then to the Saarland? I see her endearing yet severe face for the last time, now completely bewildered.

We walk across the square to the massed people. Hollow faces which show signs of deprivation but glow from the inside, hungry eyes, and above them billboards for mobile phones and the latest instant soups. Since dreams need to be manufactured, adverts are brought into a country first, then the goods.

The men stare silently. They have every reason to be suspicious, of everybody who comes and wants something: their country, profit, military influence, their women, their dignity? What good thing has ever come from abroad since they've been around? And at the same time they don't know our most normal actions. They inspect everything, decoding our life through our routines. How do we blow our noses? When do we touch one another as we speak? How do we make a suitcase roll?

At the railing of a fenced-off area Nadia's cousin Mirwais is waiting. He'll be our guide and take care of us. A reserved, bearded man in a grey one-piece Afghan suit, carrying in his hand the prayer beads, the tasbeeh, that he'll barely put down for a minute during the whole trip.

Mirwais has a face that can't look serious without suffering. That makes his sudden bursts of laughter all the more pleasing. His eyes dart around, reading the surroundings. He was a mujaheddin himself for a long time, and a radio presenter and a journalist before he turned away from politics in disillusionment and started to manage what was left of Nadia's family's properties. He's also a close friend and helper of the Afghanischer Frauenverein (Afghan Women's Organization, a German NGO). In the coming weeks we'll hear everyone speak about him with respect.

Arrival in a trauma, in an Old Testament landscape, for many people the embodiment of death and devastation, in which people disappear, kick the bucket, bite the dust, will be missed forever. Forever. A country living in the shadow of everything that's missing.

Its history of war dominates everything. The last rocket attack was only a few weeks ago, burnt-out tanks and heavy equipment lie stranded. Even road workers in a ditch hold their spades like weapons. And children lean on house walls, in eerily adult poses that they've copied from fighters. In the luxury of our psychology we call it 'traumatization'. To put it another way – they have wrestled their life from death and haven't yet won it back completely.

Your eye gathers up clues that support what you already know, or thought you knew. The ruins, the crosses, the grave mounds with fluttering flags, the weapons, the bullet holes, the scorched patches. Who's still affected by that? Who isn't numb yet? The others, who carry it all with them: grave mounds in their eyes. It's buried itself in the folds around their eyes, modelled their physiognomies.

Kabul Airport, long fought over, is today flanked by a lorry graveyard, abandoned positions, the wrecks of aeroplanes and smashed up helicopters in collapsing hangars. Every plane that touches down here in the misery of this ruined city is greeted by three giant hoardings of representatives: President Karzai, the war hero Massud and Siemens – Welcome to Kabul.

At the side of the road there's a rocket as a memorial, while old storage containers accommodate shops selling vegetables, hanging meat and Everest Pizza. The architecture of misery is the same the world over.

Hot on the heels of peace come the mobile phone traders. Buses, taken out of service in Germany and donated to the Kabulis, greet us with 'Modern Hamburg All the Best'. We pass military checkpoints, then the Ministry for Borders and Tribal Matters, then the Clinic for War Victims. Welcome to Kabul.

~

The story of Afghanistan, which has never been colonized, is one of a continual fight to maintain independence. What will come of the nation's pride now that it is being pushed into a culture that's not its own, into Western democracy, world trade, the Internationale of entertainment and fast food?

Guns, opium and the burka are also part of Afghan culture. Is that to be denied? The poppy had its part in rituals, in medicine. It was added to tea, and it even became a weapon at some point in the war against the Soviets. During the Soviet occupation in the Eighties the fields were enlarged and some Soviet soldiers fell victim first to addiction, and then to the bullets of the mujaheddin.

The old fight for self-preservation continues. A third of the population may say that 'disarmament' is a condition for peace, but guns are part of the land's traditions, its male traditions. Women didn't abuse the burka to smuggle weapons, even in times of war. By now disarmament has only had a real impact on heavy arms. People talk proudly of nearly 40,000 disarmed militiamen. But some of them join splinter groups, insurgents and revisionists. Guns are still widespread, and every day there's news of more stockpiles.

After September 11th, the West greeted the bombing of Kabul almost blindly as a cathartic action, and promised reconstruction. If a third of the population believe in disarmament, only 2 per cent place their trust in 'help from outside', and that in spite of a presence of almost 2,000 international NGOs.

Without them, however, and the aid of its exiles, the country's disaster would be complete. Yet even exiles who put their money and lives into helping the country are often mocked as 'dog cleaners' who washed the rich Westerners' curs, had an easy, prosperous life and left those back home in the lurch. The pride, and stubbornness, of the Afghans who stayed doesn't permit anything else.

~

Here and there in front of the grey rocks are the orange dots of tangerine sellers. They are importers, brokers and middlemen. Afghans have always been traders more than producers, that's their skill. But their nuts and dried fruits sometimes exceed the West's regulations on pesticide levels and then the local traders can't off-load their goods, or can only export them to India.

Now that the country's elections are behind it and it's experiencing the first months of a fragile peace, it has to beg for the cheapest kind of charity: the Western world's interest. But the spotlight has moved elsewhere.

We hear that only 6 per cent of people in Afghanistan have electricity. We'll be among them. A quarter of all children don't survive to the age of five. We put on sympathetic expressions. Even in Kabul itself 80 per cent of the people rely on outside help. We distribute alms. Half of the population is chronically malnourished.

'I can't see anyone here starving,' I hear a European saying.

Five per cent have been left disabled by the wars or mines. We express our regret. It carries on like this, but the facts are just empty words if you haven't seen it.

~

The hotel room's only decoration is an A4 photo of tourists on deck chairs in front of bamboo huts. The inscription underneath says 'Afghanistan'. I've never imagined the country like that. Outside the muezzin calls. The bed cover is made of velour, covered with big roses.

Step inside and quickly memorize the routes around the room. Power cuts come without warning, so soon you'll have to find your way in the dark.

Night is of a different material here too, full of the gazes of those who stare wide-eyed into it, they can't do anything else but stare and keep watch. An atmosphere like the slow uncurling of the fingers of a fist as fear subsides, or when death comes.

The fear that we feel as travellers, and the fear that lay like lead over the city for decades. All kinds of fear collide, at the moment there are added fears of earthquakes and of cholera.

~

The doorman has an empty stare when he doesn't know he's being watched, or rather: he stares at emptiness. Later he says that he was advised to wear flesh-coloured socks. As his skin is yellow though, he chose yellow ones. They really don't show up.

He kneels down in the hotel garden next to an armed guard who has propped his Kalashnikov up against a bush. The fighters' expressions change when they pray. Some become gentle.

If one of them had been a Talib or had collaborated with them, how would he view the world now, where Nadia walks down the street without a veil, where Christian wanders among the crowds with his camera, past kiosk shutters plastered with photos of women, past women on election posters? And why, even for foreigners, are so many things associated with the 'time of the dark beards'?

After the publication of his novel *Earth and Ashes* Atiq Rahimi became the most famous contemporary Afghan author abroad, but in Afghanistan, a country without any publishers, he's still unknown. During the Taliban era he asked, 'How can we describe the present except as oppression? It is this oppression that makes us doubt our existence, that drives us to seek refuge in our dreams.' Gradually, his train of thought continues, people believe 'their dreams more than reality! How else could all these revolutions, all these wars and all these ideologies become reality?'

And then the rebirth of creativity in disobedience, the Résistance in children's games: flying kites was prohibited under the Taliban, but the kites couldn't be kept down. Sometimes children just tied them to something, so that they could dance across the sky, ownerless but no less real for it.

Imagine what it means to be constantly fighting. The pain is a collective experience. Every second male hand that you shake will have killed. Every family has known terrible loss, and has had its own fighters and victims.

They fought the British first, who had to retreat from Kabul in shame in 1842, then the Soviets, who retreated in 1989, then factions from their own country and then the Taliban and the Americans. Now they're stepping into the space that they wanted to win back. It's called peace. What do they do? Puzzled expressions, a smile. For now women and children are excluded.

~

To cultivate atmosphere you don't ask for or request anything, you don't get straight to the point, you encircle it, you adorn it, you unroll a carpet, take a few nuts and some dried fruit, convey a feeling of ease and a willingness to spend a lifetime in the presence of those around you.

Perhaps you let your point be half-glimpsed. You wait with any request until just before you leave. Goal-orientated, result-driven Western pragmatism lacks culture. Waiting implies that there must be something worth sharing and saying in the end.

~

In a country without the sea the colour blue has a different meaning. Here it shines with the sky, the burka and lapis lazuli.

A land in the colours of emery paper, now a coarse yellow, now fine as sand. Even the green of tanks and the camouflage of Western uniforms look bright here.

And the exoticism of Western objects in these surroundings: a torch with a built-in spirit level, multi-purpose trousers with five different pockets on each leg, an indoor fountain, the picture of a gingerbread house.

In our luggage we have medical equipment for a midwifery project in Qolab in Shakardara district: examination light, blood pressure monitor, pelvimeter, uterine sound, stethoscope, reflex hammer, operating scissors, episiotomy scissors, curette. Afghanistan is the country with the highest mortality rates in childhood and childbirth.

~

The country's wounds are visible. Fighters arrive on makeshift crutches and false legs crudely hammered together at home. Their clothes and cars are adorned with scrap from the war. A goldfinch cheeps in a cage, mangy dogs wander between walls. Incapable of working the fields, the mutilated warriors limp to Peshawar in Pakistan, buy goods and then flog them on the local market.

And what a market! A crossroads for everything that can be meant by the phrase 'the exchange of wares'. In the sluggishly moving mass of people there are porters with building materials, with bird cages, cooked sheep's heads, pink plastic guns, fish and animal waste. Sometimes the bundles of goods seem to move through the crowd on their own, but underneath them men and animals are bent double, handcarts and wagons groan.

Right beside this is a two-storey loggia that was twice plundered and set alight by the Taliban. The money market, the centre of the unofficial currency exchange, reserved for men only. They stand between cracked staircases, under ceilings that have lost some of their stonework, holding onto half-broken banisters with two fingers of one hand and balancing piles of money in their other arm, weighing them afterwards on scales, and carrying them in travel bags and metal boxes.

The mobile phone stands have been built in the dry bed of the river Kabul. There customers wind their way from stall to stall between dumped rubbish, looking for the best price for long-distance calls. Then they turn away and crouch over the sound of a voice for a long time before resurfacing.

Many injured people walk around the dilapidated stage of this bazaar, and many a dressed-up little child looks bewilderedly from black-lined eyes at the confusion. The eyeliner is supposed to protect against the evil eye, and against all the other dangers that rise from the depths of this market.

~

People mill around a restaurant, drawn by the promise of relief from their weakness, bustling around, sniffing things out, a restless scurrying like just before a storm breaks, or panic. Once inside, animalistic behaviour at the feeding spots – they spread out, look around and flare their nostrils, all as a prelude to fighting for a piece of the pie, wiping their mouths and licking their lips. They plead and threaten, ask and devour. There's something intimate about watching people satisfy basic needs.

~

Back in the Twenties under King Amanullah, equal rights for women and men were established. Women were granted access to all public spaces, including cinemas, theatres and cafés, which they could also go to unattended by men. In the Sixties they even went to bars, danced with strangers, sat with their female friends in restaurants and sat in parliament. They led emancipated lives.

And now let us be clear about the radicalism of the change

that happened over a few months. It began with fighting between the armies of irregulars in the Nineties. Their commanders represent different tribes and ethnic peoples. The Tajik hero was Shah Massud, still omnipresent today. The hero of the Pashtuns: Abdul Haq, who – legend has it – fought with a prosthetic limb. General Dostum and his Uzbek troops laid waste to Kabul. They plundered and raped, they murdered.

When the Taliban routed Dostum in April 1996, they were welcomed with open arms. Their early measures seemed designed to make public spaces safe again. Then women's education was stopped. They were also prohibited from wearing high heels because the clicking sound was said to disturb the peace. Games of football were banned. Televisions and videos were confiscated, and windows had to be painted black so that women couldn't be seen from outside.

It's worth noting that there's the Taliban's Islam, an Arab-influenced one, and then the philosophical Islam that around two-thirds of all Afghans are adherents of and that, along with the codes of honour and tribal law, was the actual moulding influence on Afghan culture. The Taliban's Islam was learnt in Pakistan's Koranic schools, and developed in the refugee camps. It was a kind of rebellion of the uneducated. Its simplicity suited illiteracy.

Soon the Taliban came to control 90 per cent of the country. Early support from the United States and diplomatic recognition from the United Arab Emirates, Pakistan and Saudi Arabia gave it political legitimacy.

Women's prisons were soon full to bursting. Public whippings and stonings took place in stadiums. The male world triumphed in a kind of macho totalitarianism. It wasn't by chance. The Taliban, too, knew Western films and media, their leaders had been in the United States, they had travelled the world. They knew the attitudes from which they were protecting Afghanistan, and they could take credit for the dramatic drop in criminality. In a country accustomed to war, that was no small matter. But at what price?

And on the other hand, what do we in the West have to offer instead? We turn everything into a marketplace, devaluing non-material things, although they are at the core of a culture. Selling off the virtues that (both Islamic and non-Islamic) Afghan society values is fundamentalist in its own way and provokes a fundamentalist answer.

The traditions of classical Afghan music used to be found concentrated in Kharabat, a single district of Kabul. Before the war musicians, instrument makers and music teachers were trained here in a tradition handed down from generation to generation for over a hundred years. There was lively exchange and mutual development, the knowledge of traditional music was preserved.

Yet the quarter was completely destroyed, including its music archives, the foundations for the traditions that were passed on orally. Today many singers and musicians have returned from Iran and Pakistan. They scrape together a living from teaching, circumcision ceremonies and engagement and wedding parties. Even at these events it's not easy for traditional music. Boys with synthesizers and sound systems have taken over, some of them just play cassettes.

Once night has fallen we go to a cultural centre in the old musicians' quarter where tonight three musicians will play for the city's artists. The centre is in the spare local style reminiscent of Neue Sachlichkeit architecture. The façade is finely structured, its windows skilfully placed and accentuated by flat bands and ledges. When you see such a building, you suspect how foreign the pompous, baroque Pakistani-style palaces must look to Afghans. Yet that's the kind of house the warlords, drug barons and homecomers from the Pakistani refugee camps prefer. The ex-refugees don't know anything else.

Gestures play between the musicians. The inconspicuous one plies his trade like an old craftsman, his body language expresses his professional responsibility; next to him sits the grand seigneur – a virtuoso who can't surprise himself any more but who mimes appreciative comments left and right; on the far side is the youngest one, aflame with his ideas, he has to laugh, seeing himself constantly overtaken by his own fingers' dexterity, he throws back his head in amazement, plays a Yes! to the heavens, laughs, and again a Yes!

~

You question your own culture. How do I move, how do I smile, when do I touch a person I'm talking to? Is my style of conversation frontal, confrontational, evasive or ornamental? How do I respond when I'm given something? Do I keep my promises? What do I say to console someone? Nothing that we would call psychological has the same meaning here. Everybody appears to be simultaneously coarse and deep, superficial and flighty. What we find touching, an Afghan storyteller won't dwell on; what shocks us, doesn't affect him. Written works are almost unavailable now, but the attitude has remained.

One says, 'The Americans have only had electricity for 120 years. We've had culture for 4,000 years.'

You can recognize a country by its blessings and curses too. The curses: 'You lice-ridden beard never touched by a comb, like a road sweeper's broom!', 'Let the body washer take you!' The blessings: 'Let your blessed shadow never depart from your head!', 'Let your horoscope be fortunate!'

Who says to their daughter, 'your place is under a burka'? Who would wish to have a woman under a hive with a peep hole, as Robert Byron in the Thirties wrote of the burka? Who would wish that women look at the world out of cloth prisons, through woven bars? And how does the world look from there?

So, who didn't wear one? The nomads, who dress differently; the farm girls, who needed practical clothes in the fields; and the elite, who were westernized. However, it would be hard to find a rural housewife who doesn't wear the burka, even today. The men joke, 'Have you seen this stunning woman?'

'How do you know she's beautiful?'

'The way she holds herself!'

'And how do you recognize your wife?'

'I always choose her shoes for her.'

The four million refugees from Afghanistan who still live abroad also carry a burka. It's invisible, but everything they see appears as a fuzzy image, compared to the country they have left.

Kabul lies at an altitude of 5,900 feet, and yet the surrounding mountains rise so high above the bowl of the city that they seem to come straight out of the sea. But none of those alpine meadows and sloping pastures here! They tower up from dust and rock – not a landscape for observers, nor for inhabitants, rather one in which all human presence seems incidental, if not unwelcome. Their features are clear and reduced to the elemental. Local art, however, is an utter contrast. Its ornamental forms create an extravagant and fanciful effect.

In our part of the world we aren't used to seeing culture after it has fallen into decline. Our cities are more and more efficient machines, and the first thing they do is to eradicate past eras of decline. The destruction is only preserved in museums. Seen in this way, Kabul presents an urban form that we don't know: expansion in the midst of destruction.

A dusty city inhaling fine sand, wrapped in smog, wafting exhaust fumes, battered and bursting at the seams. This city, which was designed for under a million inhabitants, today has a good four million. It has no sewerage system, just drainage ditches full of rubbish that stink each summer, electricity from the grid for only about a quarter of the population, the rest rely on generators as unpredictable as the television reception. There's the threat of cholera, earthquakes, suicide bombers, muggings, enemy sniping, of Taliban attacks and of arguments between different ethnicities being re-kindled.

And yet flowers are being planted, vines hang on espaliers and songbirds twitter in cages. Anything people have ever found poetic is even more poetic here, hard won as it is against the nature of the times. Wasps, butterflies and coal tits dart through the trees by the clinic for war victims. Men lie underneath the trees as if still sedated, on this last day of Ramadan.

Kabul is growing rapidly as more and more refugees return home. A major new city is already being planned for the north, to relieve the pressure on Kabul.

Its ugliest area of growth has been nicknamed Warlord City. A district of unfinished shells of houses, financed by blood money and built in the exaggeratedly ornate Pakistani style, it's the warlords' luxury ghetto, despised by everyone else.

Warlords buy front men to stand in elections, people already talk about the puppet MPs, while the candidate who brought up the issue of divorce was barred from running, as his proposals were said to infringe Islamic law.

Warlord City is deserted. As if a reminder of its residents' past, three burnt-out tanks are piled on top of one another at the side of an unpaved road.

An American aid worker complains in passing that the beggars on Chicken Street always reel off their stories so monotonously. Does he think the beggars should make an effort to act their character without letting the routine show? But what if they are so obsessed by this one story that it can't be altered, especially as it's so many people's story?

A former resident of the refugee camp in Peshawar tells us that he knew women there who only talked about plastic surgery. The last refuge of a desire to change things is your own body. It's within your reach. After mobile phones, gyms will arrive, along with cosmetic surgeons. This too is a sign of how differently exiles were brought up.

Nadia is in the hotel foyer, on the phone to Mirwais, who

still has to buy a few things at the bazaar: 'Mirwais, hold the phone out a minute, I want to hear the bazaar!'

Aghaniyar: a term that covers love of the homeland, pride in it, a valuing of local life, and the Afghans' close ties to their homeland. By now it's part of a culture which even separates the exiled Afghans from the non-exiles. It makes a difference whether you're homesick for a country you can't see, or love it while despairing at its daily reality.

~

Among the candidates in the elections is an Afghan woman who has returned from exile in provincial Germany. She has four children there but finds the work in her homeland too vital for her just to watch from a distance. Many people vote for her, and others try to buy these votes. There are rumours that even the UN is working to buy votes for the US. Trust evaporates, people just smile wryly at the election monitors, and experts estimate that the country's new democratic constitution has a 50 per cent chance of succeeding. If it doesn't, the warlords, drug barons and front men will take control.

~

The US base in the city has five lines of defence around it, made of concrete blocks, stone obstacles, high walls and barbed wire. Over the months new walls are added, the latest encircles all the others as protection against suicide bombers.

This is war too: we're experiencing the birth of a state, it's about water supplies, hygiene, transport, electricity, logistics and infrastructure.

First, mosques are repaired and bunkers prepared.

A large open space on the edge of the city, dotted with football goals among which cows are grazing. Whimpering music from somewhere. Rolled in dust, the street children's hair sticks up in spikes, each strand turned grey with dust. Some are carrying high-heeled sandals, half-eaten flat bread or an empty canister.

I've never seen children's faces like these. They're at once childish, getting swept up in bouts of wild excitement, and at the same time old, with dark rings under their eyes and wrinkles around their mouth. Old women in children's bodies – their eyelashes mascaraed with dust. In this area of about half a square mile, they pounce on each new visitor with their shoeblack boxes and the water canisters from which they refill people's drinking bottles. Sometimes they're just curious or hoping to bag something. They might be eight years old, often younger, but they already know all about pity, shoe repairs and the art of survival.

Kabul's big stadium is hidden behind a concrete building on the other side of the field. To earn a few pennies, the children are allowed to bring water for the athletes. They bought their bread from foreign soldiers for five afghani. It's enough to ward off their own hunger for now.

These children live far away, but they see their best chance of survival in the seething city. Every morning they take the minibus for two afghani. If they can't pay they get two slaps round the face and are left behind.

'Do you know the football women who train here?'

'We've even been in their offices.'

The leader looks boldly at us. He knows all the women's

and men's teams' results, he'd liked to have played himself, 'but my dad's dead, and I have to help support my family.'

We let him take us into the stadium, a ramshackle place. He watches us. 'It looks dirty to you,' he says, 'but it's paradise to me.'

In the training building two men are running circuits in a room of 25 square feet that's laid out with mats.

'They're boxers,' the little boy says, awe-struck.

Upstairs, a warm welcome from the Afghan trainer of the women's team and the German supervisor. The German is 'football crazy', his black moustache and Adidas jacket make him look like he's straight out of Germany's football scene in the Seventies. The Afghan trainer is just as enthusiastic, his friendliness floats on a deeper mourning. He travels all around the country scouting out talent, making an effort to coach in other regions too. He's just returned from the north where only half a year ago a woman was stoned. Football is an answer too.

We're led into a room that is surrounded on two sides by closed curtains, almost giving the effect of standing in a tent. It's hung with posters of the three times Women's World Footballer of the Year, Birgit Prinz, who recently led a training course for the women here. She quickly won their friendship and respect. Physically she looks like a fighting machine in comparison to the three petite, perhaps undernourished women players who now enter the room. The first has sweaty hands and an east Asian face largely covered by a veil; the second has the raw skin and red face of those who sleep outside; the third is a porcelain-fragile lady with finely drawn features and turquoise make-up, her veil has slipped and she flirts innocently. These are three of the leading women footballers, picked from the eleven clubs in Kabul who will soon be fighting it out against teams from three other Afghan provinces.

It's hoped that one day an Afghan women's national team will be formed from the group of 14–18 year olds who are being trained together. The girls' most important quality is their ability to assert their passion for football against the doubts of society and their families. And how difficult conditions are! It's almost impossible to train at home, there's no room. In public spaces, where men can gape, they aren't allowed to play. As a result, until now none of the games have been open to the public. The girls train in full-length tracksuit trousers, but with short-sleeved shirts and without their veils.

This is a success. A few months ago they were still training in their veils, and more freedom just wouldn't be accepted yet. Now part of the burden of having women's sports accepted in public rests on the narrow shoulders of these women, in a society where women have been hidden for so long.

One of the girls trained with her brothers before registering. Now her heading skills are better than her footwork.

'And do you play hard, do you ever foul?'

'I've been fouled a lot, but never been sent off myself. Others have. They're always getting yellow cards, and sometimes red.' Every little thing that makes the game normal is a cause for celebration.

'We prefer players who have great personalities,' the trainer adds. 'A good player needs to set a good example, particularly in this unusual sport. Also, a good player has to give her all, doing just what her trainer says.'

One of the players learnt to play in a Pakistani refugee camp. She had been watching a game, getting really annoyed at the players, and wanted to play herself.

'So we all chipped in for a ball, and it went from there. Two girls had really good skills, and that spurred others on. They started playing too and gradually we had a whole a team.' She concludes like an expert: 'Because one was good, the others got interested.'

In order to train, the girls need support from their families. Their parents need to be brave, face ill will and help their daughters to stay motivated. Not easy when the training is hours away – scary hours sometimes, the journey can be dangerous. The girl that cycled for two hours to get here today was pelted with stones and banana peel on her way.

Aggression aimed at their sport? Symptoms of war trauma? Who can say? Everything here is watched closely – whether they wear make-up, put on lipstick, play in shorts, take off their veils, everything is commented on. For that reason alone the girls can only train indoors, their game improves slowly and they feel the lack of international competitions. As tender as they seem, they have to bear enormous psychological pressure to train. It's good that this weekend there's a friendly game in Turkmenistan.

There's a framed photo of the FIFA president Sepp Blatter, FIFA pennants and medals in a glass display cabinet, and a lapis lazuli globe beside them. In some way these trophies and decorations are the insignia of their entry into world football. How they long for public appearances, trips, stadiums with full terraces, and yet it's so far off. I turn to the red-faced girl. 'Is your father a football fan?'

'No, he's dead. But my mother is proud. So I'm allowed to train at home with my cousins. They throw me balls.' She has deep, chesty cough.

It's impossible not to ask about their families, impossible to ask, knowing that the dead wait in every answer. As they're always apologizing for their mistakes, I try a different tack, that of the admiring chronicler with an outsider's view of things.

'Just think,' I say. 'You're pioneers. Everything starts with you. One day your photos will be in books. That's where Afghan women's football started, people will say, looking at a picture on the first page of you all as you are now. They'll say: Look at their shoes, their shirts, they still wore veils then, and tracksuit trousers! You're preparing the path.'

They don't understand the 'path'. The future is somehow unimaginable.

Less so for the trainer. Everything depends on him, on his ability to have his way in spite of male opposition, to enthuse people, and on his resourcefulness. He tours the city's districts tirelessly, visiting families, looking out for talent and measuring the extent to which women's football can be made public.

He has a subversive strategy. Firstly the team trained in secret, then the first press releases went out. It's only been a year now that the general public has known of the existence of women's football in Afghanistan. It still needs to be convinced, just as the players' families did before they gave their approval.

'We'd do anything for our trainer,' the girls say. 'Anything. When he calls, we come, wherever we are.'

He listens to them, shows them training videos to teach them heading and dribbling. He tries to appear strict.

They get out pictures of the whole team. Pretty young women in blue and red whose faces show how much courage they need to represent this sport in public. They're sometimes intimidated by the strong reactions to what they are doing.

I talk shop with the trainer, he likes that. 'What formation do you play?'

'4-4-2. We're better attacking than in defence.'

The girls look as if they're surprised to already be part of a 'formation'. Their footballing knowledge is partial. They don't have a clear notion of the different strategies available to a team, but they look up to Ronaldinho, Ronaldo, and Michael Ballack, too.

'Who will win the World Cup?'

Two say Brazil, one Germany. What does the trainer think?

'If Germany carry on like they're playing now, they haven't got a chance.'

Sometimes the girls play against young boys from the streets of Kabul. The boys are fast and have good stamina.

'And you aren't afraid of getting fat legs from all the football?'

They giggle. 'If we were, we wouldn't have got this far. When we run onto the pitch we're prepared to lose. But we always give our best. So we can't worry about our legs.'

'Do you have any special rituals before the games?'

Do they ever. One reads certain verses of the Koran, another lights a candle and eats dried fruit, 'because you forget your problems when you're eating'. A third prays.

'And your battle cry?'

All together they shout, 'We want to work together like the fingers of a hand!'

Then they grab their handbags, proffer a friendly, if not insistent, invitation to a meal, and leave. Just 20 yards further on, at the main road, no one would suspect that the hope of Afghan football is found in these three teenagers.

The 'paradise' stadium that the little boy told us about has damaged, but decorated, terraces, in the shadow of portraits of Karzai, Massud and past militia commanders. Large pools of water lie on the pitch and the running track. Burnt patches can be seen in the places where drugs were once burnt publicly. I had seen the stadium in Saira Shah's documentary – a horrific place of show trials and executions.

'Sometimes we saw victims strung up on the goalposts,' the trainer says. 'Women in their burkas were whipped and stoned here, and over there, where the grass doesn't grow any more, people were shot. And they told us all to come and watch. The upper terraces were for women only.'

He starts to point upwards but halfway loses the strength to finish the gesture.

'They stood up there, with guards around them. The mullah stood in front of the stands with a microphone and stated what the crime and what the punishment were. He gave his judgment. Then a member of the victim's family was given a revolver and made to shoot the victim, not with a single shot, but with three, in the head, chest and stomach. Some of the family members went so crazy that they didn't stop shooting, out of fear of doing something wrong.'

The trainer can barely say these things. His wife, we hear in passing, also trains a team. At that time he went home to her and fell ill. He can't explain it more precisely. He just fell ill. He's seen a lot.

'Believe me. We're so happy that we survived and can now work – by playing!'

Terrible depths lurk between each sentence. The pitch is a muddy field full of puddles, and behind the corner flag nothing grows – there's just a large dark stain.

'We tried all year to sow grass over there, where the people were shot. But it won't grow. It won't grow.'

He turns his face away. It's like a late summer's day in the arena. When a military jet passes overhead everyone looks up.

When it's said that someone's wearing white, it means that he's wearing his burial cloth and is ready to die. Green flags mark out the martyrs on the graveyard hillocks. Most of them died fighting the Russians.

A Thursday evening on the edge of the city. Up to the right are the ruins of the gigantic castle that the British destroyed in the 19th century. To the left a wide low-lying area with football goals, sparsely growing grass and small groups of children kicking balls around. One rides away on a three-legged goat. Another searches for matches in the sand. A third creates arabesque lines as he pushes a wheelbarrow around, sunk in thought.

Near them men are washing their cars before the holy day, using water that they pump from the deep holes at the side of the road. This all occurs in the shadow of the cemeteries that spread out on the hillside between houses and ruins, for people live here among the dead and the graves dotted with clumps of flags.

There are many holy sites in this area, some of the early holy men and martyrs were buried here. From here you can even see the place from which Islam spread in Afghanistan. The first believers were killed there by fire worshippers. Today fire worshippers are present as a dwindling minority, but Islam is alive in a wide variety of currents, from liberal to fundamentalist ones.

When it was founded, between 610 and 632, the ancient world was dying and a new age was arriving. Christianity had spread south to Central Arabia. So Islam, as the youngest of the world religions, developed in the light of the new times' awakening understanding, and in an area between Mecca and Medina strong in Jewish and Christian influences. It didn't only know of them, it sucked them up and so they are alive in Afghanistan to this day.

The foundations of the old castle are from the pre-Islamic era, and the settlements in its shadow and on the mountainside opposite are also old. The hard life of their residents seems eternal. 'A hard life,' Mirwais says, but in his mouth it has a heavier ring. We see people carrying their drinking water on their backs up the mountain, we see the slope turning black as night falls, while in other quarters lights come on here and there like candles.

From down on the big field we can hear music from car radios. Foot mats are being cleaned. Dogs slurp up water from soapy buckets and from the little puddles that are collecting rain and carwash water.

Further off a single man is riding round in circles on his donkey. Above him kites are flying. Gradually the chugging of generators kicks in behind the radio music and a night begins in which no one can think of entertainment. It's the last day of Ramadan. Everybody seems slow, cooled down, their gaze focused on Eid, the three-day festival that makes relatively modest demands: do more good, say a special prayer, eat with your family, receive visitors, be a guest and show hospitality

– that's about it. Eid is also celebrated by lighting fireworks. People are constantly being startled.

We walk up to one of the shrines. The steps are lined with praying supplicants: lovesick, or otherwise sick, men; burka-wearing beggars; women who dare to touch us but are then sent packing by others. I stare into one of these windows to a face – behind it an ageless but made-up pair of eyes.

~

In the market fish are being smoked. In the street a beggar wearing a burka holds her newborn child out into the blue clouds of exhaust smoke. The child's bloated head swells out of its brightly coloured woollen clothes. Nadia stops. 'Why are you poisoning your child?'

'It's mine.'

'But it will die in these fumes.'

'It's my child, and I don't have anything to eat!'

We give something. The hand the beggar stretches out is ancient. Probably she's only hired the child for her begging. This *pietà* is there every day we pass by. The burka protects female beggars from their own shame.

~

Beggars also weave through the traffic jam like cleaner fish, supplying the four lanes of cars, as well as directing and blocking them. In the middle of it all a camel, a couple of horses. A boy has fresh bolani in his cart – a kind of turnover filled with potatoes and a spicy sauce. Night is falling. Christian and I buy ourselves a handful and eat as we walk. The boy passes his goods to drivers stuck in the jam. Opposite him a boy of about the same age is just getting out of his oven. Sitting in a walled dome, he reaches further in with a shovel and extracts finger bread that will be sold immediately. Another boy grabs it and folds it like a gentleman's handkerchief. 'Come,' one of the beggars calls out to us. 'Come into my oven.'

They're sitting around the fire, their faces as dark as charcoal burners in fairy tales.

A gaunt innkeeper with the soul of a missionary ambles out of the back of his inn. Wrapped in cloths, as thin as after a pack march, wearing a pakul hat on his head.

'I was a mujaheddin,' he says straight off. 'And I welcome you.' His left hand goes to his heart.

'I was Massud's friend, was at his side …' He walks over to the wall. A small framed picture shows him on a horse, beside Massud.

'I was with him in the Panjshir Valley. We built an irrigation plant too. Here.' The photo shows the loop of a river. The former mujaheddin traces the semi-circle of the irrigation plant with his finger, a system of channels and pipes parallel to the bending river.

'And now sit down. I've slaughtered a young lamb. You've come to the right place. A clean lamb. We'll eat it.'

As we eat he continues to talk politics. 'You Germans are the most popular. Your work is good. You have concentrated on supplying electricity and training the police though, while the British have fought the opium trade. Maybe you'd be less popular if you'd had that job to do.'

I ask him about the regularly promised reduction in opium growing. He knows better. There was a surplus of opium last year, the stores are still full. That's the only reason why less has been planted this year.

'Every country helps,' he says, with presidential airs. 'That's good. But they don't all help in a sustainable way. Some only think of their own business interests. The Japanese wanted to help with the bus network, but they've withdrawn. The Chinese and Turks take money for road building projects, and you Germans, why don't you plant forests? There isn't enough firewood. And there's a dam. You built it yourselves. Now it's broken. If you rebuild it, you'll help 10,000 people. Tell that to your ambassador.'

I promise that I will, and when I later really am sitting with the ambassador, who appears to be well informed and courageous, I dutifully bring up the topic. His assistant takes some notes on the case and is asked to look into it immediately.

Then I go back to Massud's friend and tell him that the ambassador is already working on the dam's rebuilding. Shortcut politics. It's nothing new to him, he nods and thanks me. From the back of the room more young, clean lamb is already being brought to me.

The Russians' and the Americans' campaigns have both been largely from the air, killing over a million civilians in the process. For decades the Afghans were the skilled fighters, proud that no one could match their skills in man-to-man combat: the Russians weren't agile enough, and the Americans were too fat to climb the mountains.

The Afghans value their independence above all else, at the moment particularly independence from Western invaders, even from aid organizations, but also from the increasing pressure from Pakistan and Iran. To face up to these powers the Afghans more or less privatized their military, by placing power in the hands of tribal chiefs and mercenary commanders. It was a way of earning your living, and absurd as it sounds, now that the country is on or already over the threshold of a new era, some people don't really know what to do now, how to find work and live without fighting. Is a time approaching when some will say that things were better during the war?

On the other hand people's current satisfaction can be seen in the fact that some are now strong enough to imagine the misery of the Russian soldiers who were sent to the inhospitable south as cannon fodder, to kill and to die.

There's just no country where you won't initially be amazed at how patient the soldiers, workers and little people are, and at how unable they are to get indignant about their situation and organize themselves.

A beggar limps out of the flow of traffic, blood on the mesh of her burka. Behind it her lips move, painted blood red, but three shades lighter.

Those who control the traffic are the ones who limp, come up to you on crutches, roll along legless on little carts – the injured, disabled and reduced. They're a continual memory of those who aren't ready to head into a new era, who will be carried along in the flow if they're lucky. If the visible injuries are transposed onto inner lives, and we imagine all the mental scars too, it becomes clear that this is a city of crippled people.

In front of Kabul's orthopaedic centre the half-dead and injured who have dragged themselves here from the provinces lie waiting. They lie there with their crutches and look out into the traffic with eyes that no longer look for their missing legs.

~

The history contained in faces, their saturation with experience. People who have experienced too much. It's too serious for them to hold it back, it floods out in their expressions. And then: a willingness to speak poetry, and to feel it as such.

~

Cholera has broken out in Kabul. The city picks an epidemic that suits it. The coming threat looks like this: the ditches are open sewers and animals wander freely, so when summer arrives and a miasma hangs in the alleys, then the stinking air will carry bacteria and viruses, then new epidemics will bloom.

~

In the evening we meet human rights activists, doing their best to help, but in a losing battle. And yet, we've heard so much about Afghanistan's courageous women – about the film-maker who even in the Taliban era filmed from under her burka, the many teachers who gave girls lessons secretly at night, the founder of the first free radio station under the Taliban, about the first person to openly demand in the tribal assembly, the Loya Jirga, that warlords and drug barons be prosecuted, and about the only woman among the 17 candidates in the presidential election.

Djamila, a human rights activist, is one of these modern Afghan women – though not 'modern' as Western women's magazines understand it. She wears the veil, and has a pronounced limp. She's the first woman from her village to have studied at university, the first to become politically engaged, and disillusioned. The Afghans want democracy, she tells us. 'But so early and on these conditions? It hasn't grown from us.'

Yet Djamila still travels from village to village, urging the Afghan women to vote.

'Good,' they reply. 'Who would you recommend?'

'I'm not recommending anyone!' she tries to say. She's aware though, that if the farm girl doesn't ask her, she'll ask her father or brothers, fearing she'll be hit otherwise. 'Men, even my brothers, accepted violence towards women as their fate.'

And herself? Is the speed of democratization too much for her too? Her answer is heart-wrenching. 'I did everything for democratic elections, but when they came I didn't vote. No one earned my trust.'

Her phrase expresses how precious, how valuable this trust is. But how does she inform herself politically? From two minute features on the radio, like 80 per cent of the population. She can, actually, keep herself well informed about human rights issues from the 28 radio stations. About 200 daily newspapers also appear, many just a few stapled sheets, as well as 120 magazines of all kinds. There's a great interest in politics – it moulds life on a daily basis.

'When Kabul started to be bombed, after September 11th,' I say, 'people in the West justified it partly by saying it was for women's freedom.'

Djamila laughs for the first time. '*That* explanation I hadn't heard.' After a significant pause she says seriously, 'And I don't believe it either.'

Yet the country's future is here too: in Djamila, the girls in school, the women teachers, and the boys and girls learning German together at the Goethe-Institut, excited about their new start. 'I want to be a teacher, because I love other people,' one says. 'I'd like to be an interpreter for foreign soldiers.' 'I'd like to read Goethe.'

In the interests of scholarly research they've tried to talk to people in love. But that's difficult, because you're only allowed to talk about love with people who are already married. So they stage a role play in their classroom and ask each other questions.

'What is love?'

'A beautiful thing that you have to love.'

'What do you think about women and men having relationships?'

'Many people don't understand love. I've seen many have relationships in offices. I think that's good. Men can't work in society without women anyway.'

'When do you love someone?'

'When I want to.'

'How old should men and women be when they marry?'

'Women: 20, men: 30.'

'If your husband had another woman, what would you do?'

'Strangle him.'

'Will you marry the person chosen for you?'

'I'll marry the person I love.'

That's how the first youthful discussions about love sound like in Afghanistan. They are tentative attempts to struggle to find a way in the modern world, by boys and girls who still state their hobbies as knotting carpets, playing chess, forging gold, boxing and bodybuilding.

A freezing 12-year-old phonecard seller is walking home at night along the road, with – rather than against – the flow of traffic. Even so, his arm and his long ribbon of cards in plastic shoots up at the sound of every approaching car – it's automatic, not a sales pitch, there's no belief the gesture will have an effect. He does it because he's been doing it all day. This robotic blindness says more about how misery deforms people than the colourful show put on by some of the beggars. How miserably poverty forms character.

4

Nadia hands me a whole onion. She asks me to eat it, to line my stomach and arm it against everything coming its way. The next morning every dream tastes of onion.

Think of a young man who has grown up in Koranic schools in Pakistan, without any contact with women. Everything that he has learnt and been in contact with is a single, fundamentalist worldview, unquestioning and imageless. His friends are 25-year-old men from orphanages and failed mujaheddin, all disillusioned and powerless, drawing their only source of authority from their faith.

The man would know that jokes about a young Talib are common. I just hear the punchline of one: 'Your husband's head is in the garden.'

On a map of humour, the Taliban are the region's Irish. Nowadays they wear Calvin Klein and pinstripes, hoping to survive inconspicuously in the new government. A prominent Talib, for example, was held by the US in the camp at Bagram for a year. Upon his release he stood for parliament, where he now sits as a liberal. Seeing such things, the Afghans rightly ask whether re-education or just re-positioning has taken place.

But what did people think when the Taliban came to power? They welcomed many things: that they started to disarm people, that women were no longer raped, and that stability returned. Sometimes you hear people who sympathized in the past saying: yes, if only they hadn't been so radical, hadn't stirred up ethnic groups and repressed women, if they'd been less cruel, then we wouldn't have seen them as foreign invaders in our own country, we'd have been thankful for peace.

Probably every state made up of disparate ethnic groups faces its own dangers, and Afghanistan has 50 different peoples to unite – all proud, all fearing a loss of identity, and all needing to muster all the tolerance they can. Violence is a shortcut to change, and as the interior and exterior pressures have repeatedly surfaced in violence here, there's scarcely a land on earth that has experienced as many extremes over recent years.

Khaled works in a hospital lab. He's our driver too. He works at the hospital because he's passionate about medicine. As he drives, he spits with anger about what he's seen in the hospital. Because there aren't any operating lights, operations are done near windows, and people come and go in the operating theatre as they please. You can see medical students operating on open wounds after just two semesters.

The conditions are as expected. Men can't touch women, not even to position them safely on their sides. Medicines and medical equipment are sold on the black market. A Caesarean requires the husband's permission, and – if you believe rumours – he'll have bought the thread for the operation himself. Fear, depression and post-traumatic stress disorders affect the medical staff too. Foreign workers try to help people to heal psychologically as well, but who can unravel the tangled stories of suffering? Doctors often leave the hospital in the early afternoon. Helpers from abroad describe them as 'astonishingly callous'. They don't care about what they leave behind them. The war has made them all hard, hard as scar tissue.

At Eid Nadia is turquoise and gold, all embroidered hems. Her self-confidence on these feast days is magnificent, and a feast for the eyes after the weeks of hunger. We visit her in her hotel room. She looks around, saying, 'I'm sorry I can't offer you anything.' A reflex. We left the breakfast table together, just minutes earlier.

Afghanistan's kites are legendary. Firstly, glass is ground in a mortar, then kite string is soaked in glue, before being drawn through the fine splinters. Then the construction of paper and wood is released into the air and its owner tries to cut others' kite strings with his own. Whoever manages it, has to capture the plummeting, fluttering kite as a trophy.

In Germany the law states that the maximum altitude for kites is 200 metres. In Afghanistan it's infinite. The higher the kites fly, the more beautiful the sight is. We step out onto a roof. It's true, kites are always in the air somewhere. They ascend from the mud roofs, where grapes, tomatoes and aubergines are being dried.

Once a year the roofs need to be insulated with straw and earth. Roofs are where lovers traditionally meet, or from where they signal to each other from a distance. And children play on them with their kites, following their strings, jumping from roof to roof – and sometimes one of them falls between the houses. Even so, the roofs are a refuge, a different world.

~

How do Afghan men recognize their wives under their burkas, how do they know whether the women they court are attractive? The men laugh knowingly. Afghan men have developed a fine sensibility for a woman's gait. Is it graceful, is it cheeky? They see how much the women weigh. They use their imagination. And the women? They focus on the figure they cut, their naked bodily life. They often wear old clothes under the burka.

Afghan men use strong braces so that their trousers can't be pulled down. That would be a terrible disgrace.

~

The basic theme of all travel literature is how the historical changes in different ethnic groups, ways of life and areas of the world never seem to converge – to us, it appears that they develop at different speeds. There will be markedly different attitudes towards the relationship between knowledge and superstition, technology and spirituality, a desire for progress and the handing down of traditions. The traveller's first observation is therefore also about what is simultaneous and co-existent.

Storytellers still travel from village to village, captivating their audiences with simple means:

'And then a snake appeared …'

'Oh! A snake!'

'It swished over the sand.'

'Help! The sand!'

'And at night the jinn sat on their chests.'
'Mercy – the jinn!'
The same listeners can of course also use DVD players.

5

Near the Old Mosque there's a gigantic billboard for Afghan Wireless – competition for the divinities, both old and new.

Political parties haven't taken part in parliamentary elections yet, only individuals. So the city is plastered with small photocopied pictures of candidates, sometimes in colour. Above their faces, slogans such as: Prosperity, Safety, Freedom, Justice – the international promises of healing, here as there.

Due to the high level of illiteracy, next to each face there's a small symbol that will be on the voting slips too – three oil lamps, a stool, an eye, a horse. The candidates stare from the posters like wanted persons.

'Give me seats!' one candidate has written. His emblem is two wing chairs. His face seems to say he means it literally.

In the end over 60 women win seats in parliament, among them an 18-year-old. Everyone raves about how pretty she is.

A couple stood for election too. He's known to own a good racehorse. His agenda is: Religion, Science, Progress, Industry and Democracy. He doesn't win a seat. His wife's agenda isn't known, but she enters parliament.

People are in uproar about the confusion over property ownership. Some plots have been sold up to seven times in the political confusion. In the chaos of expropriations, ownership claims and murky inheritance wrangles, shady notaries and solicitors are making a killing, while civil servants, members of parliament and former warlords cherry-pick prime locations.

Meanwhile property and rental prices have been pushed up to dizzying heights, not least because of the relief organizations who all need office space and living quarters. The former owners of flats and small plots of land not only feel duped, they also find themselves exposed to a market situation that they haven't been prepared for. The coming battles will be fought out in the market economy.

We are used to traditional events in our part of the world only surviving for the tourists, and changing under their gaze. In Afghanistan festivals have survived all the years not thanks to commerce and tourism, but when they have been stronger than the war. Principal among the survivors is buzkashi, 'goat-pulling', a forerunner of polo, it is said.

It consists of a horseman snatching a dead goat or calf from the floor of an arena and trying to complete a lap while all the other riders try to steal the corpse. Fists and whips allowed. The event requires a big arena. It is wild and anarchic; it was celebrated in times of war to relieve built-up tensions.

Even in huts with just a few photos, buzkashi is the most common motif. In 50 years' time it will become Afghanistan's answer to Pamplona's Running of the Bulls, the Rhineland Carnival or Siena's Palio. We ask if we can see buzkashi anywhere at the moment. I can already imagine the horses' panicky eyes, their flared nostrils, the riders' costumes, the unrecognizable bloated corpse in their midst, and the clouds of dust. The hotelier shrugs his shoulders. Not here. Not now. Mirwais doubts that it's the right time. Maybe when we reach Kunduz.

~

There are part-time beggars too – they walk normally down the street, see a stranger, collapse immediately into a limping shuffle as they hold their hand out, and then straighten up again afterwards.

There are spiritual beggars who arrive with a little cup of coals, throw spices onto the embers and bless the giver with the incense.

One of these boys has stopped in front of a toyshop's window display, where an ear-splitting soundtrack is pumping out of Pakistani war toys. Tanks turn around, lights flash and sirens howl. Here's a plastic automatic rifle, there's a jeep with the words 'Military Force' on the side. Political reality reached this window long ago.

Standing with his incense that no one will pay for, the boy is entranced by the display. Nothing sells better on Kabul's streets than war toys from Pakistan, China and Iran. No doubt the toy manufacturers in those countries also speak of 'new markets to enter'.

~

Between a dusty race track for kids on motorbikes and a few stalls selling soup, chickpeas with potatoes and yoghurt, turnovers filled with beans and meat, coloured eggs for egg duels, and toys, rises the old military-looking Park Cinema. A pleasure palace of the past, it has survived the fighting in Kabul with hardly any external damage. Its façade has bullet marks, but they have just chipped the plaster. A few wilting, dustily grey sunflowers are growing there.

A hunchbacked guard stands at the door, frisking everyone who goes in, for weapons. The cinema tempts young men into imitating the films, so it's important to search them and make sure the imitation doesn't start right here in the cinema.

The limping guard leads us into the pitch-black room. Three women are sitting in a separate area at the back, they turn away from the beam of the torch in embarrassment.

About a hundred men have gathered in the balcony seats. They all watch a father slit open a gangster in front of the eyes of his six-year-old. Then he takes his child in his arms and the film changes genre, from action film to weepy, and back again: eight cloaked black figures are just abseiling down ropes from the roof. The men's balcony erupts in cheers. The poster advertised the film as 'Romance beyond all Dreams'.

The old picture palaces have gone to the dogs. Not many people go now, they are places of ill repute. In the Seventies Kabul's men and women went to the cinema together, families had their own boxes. During the Taliban period boys asked hairdressers furtively for the 'Titanic cut', inspired by Leonardo di Caprio. If it was found out, the hairdressers could end up in prison. Has Leonardo heard?

~

For the religious holiday a photographer has set up an artificial panorama in the park behind the cinema – a landscape with a lake and palm trees under a blue, then fiery red sky. A motorbike can also be hired and added to the décor. But today there are two men who just stand there hand in hand, and because they are both men and they know that Western men would rarely do that, they say, 'See, Afghan men are much more progressive.'

'And Afghan photographers too!' calls out the photographer, and snaps them triumphantly.

Other entertainment too: throwing hoops over cigarette packets, plastic tanks, a torch, a deck of cards and a glasses frame. The children are in their best clothes, most have scars from infections caused by lancing boils with dirty knives. This is a major complaint, along with stomach worms, parasites, typhus and malaria. The bare park gives children space to run around, but it's also where funeral services are held.

To one side a lone woman in a burka is standing by a boulder and a green pennant at the grave of a relative who was killed by the Russians. We can see she's crying because her silhouette shakes.

On one of the small hummocks a soothsayer sits under some trees looking deadly serious. On his lap he has a birdcage with three goldfinches.

'What's this bird's name?' Nadia asks.

'Bird,' replies the soothsayer.

He's wearing an Adidas cap and a flaking olive-green leather jacket. When I hand him a note he kisses his fingertips and taps on the bars of the cage with his nail. One of the three goldfinches hops over and picks a little letter from one of three little containers. The soothsayer solemnly passes me the letter. His hand has been painted red with henna. The text is a Hafiz poem, Nadia begins to translate it. 'You, who receive this prophecy. God waits in your heart. Keep impure things far from your heart, so you can see the truth …'

I'll do that. Mirwais laughs, 'Hafiz has something for everyone. He's like Karzai.'

By now a crowd of young men is listening to Nadia's German translation. The sad soothsayer looks out over the throng. He doesn't look anyone in the eye.

The park guards at their post hold their Kalashnikovs proudly and ask Christian to take their picture. He does.

'Now give me my picture!'

Can they imagine that it isn't sitting in the camera waiting to be taken out? Christian wanders off. Soon he'll disappear among the egg duellists, just as he disappears everywhere. People swarm to where he is. Then he makes himself invisible and everything is as it was before, except that his gaze still lingers in the air.

A park guard in strange, imposing sunglasses won't take his fine long-fingered hands from his weapon. 'I'm so tired of holding this thing,' he says. 'Should I drive you around instead?'

Then he takes his sunglasses off and we let out a surprised exclamation, seeing the deep emerald green of his eyes. He seems embarrassed by them, fumbles around with his belt and unsheathes his knife, an American one. The words 'Freedom Forever' are stamped on the wide blade. Suddenly the knife embarrasses him too.

'The Russian ones are better,' he says. It's the only good thing he has to say about the Russians.

An American jet roars overhead.

'Does the noise frighten you?' I ask an old man.

'The war is over. Let them fly.'

Let them fly. A few kites are also fluttering in the wind – small trapezoids of just one colour, rising from the ruins and turning in gusts of wind like flags signalling a surrender.

'The war is over, how long will you wait for the peace?'

The old man looks me directly in the eyes, 'You have the clock, we have time.'

Road signs as artwork. At a pedestrian crossing the person on the sign has no feet. Near a school a '30' speed restriction, the only traffic sign in sight. *L'art pour l'art*. A former training hall for soldiers greets us with a 'Welcoming from each Kind of Partys of Honour'. On bus and shop doors we often see 'Door', sometimes 'Welcame'.

On the street in front of the hospital the needy are waiting in long queues. They're weak, and waiting for the only doctor who holds surgery here. The street is the waiting room. When winter comes they will still be waiting out here and hoping, as long as they can.

Nadia looks silently into the distance.

'What is it?'

'I'm just remembering my year as a student at Kabul University. The café we went to was here ...'

We walk on in silence. Suddenly a bed on the pavement blocks our way. An old man sits down on it with difficulty. It's grey and sends up clouds of dust. Then a boy comes with a bouquet of bright sweet williams over his shoulder, piercing the dust they seem even more colourful, then we see buckets of flowers on the street, roses and lilies. Nadia runs over and presses her nose deep into them. When she surfaces, she looks more sober. 'Pakistani roses! They just don't smell as good as the ones from here.'

~

The cafeteria at the market is decked out in tulle. Once inside, the first thing you pass is a ramp with slaughtered animals. Two halves of cows are waiting to be cut up. Their fat has congealed to a dull yellow, the windpipe is hanging to one side and the hacked-off hooves are lying in a tin dish, covered in blood and lymph.

Mirrors and posters of landscapes, buzkashi and Massud adorn the walls, alongside fans of kebab skewers looking like medieval torture instruments. Bright orange lemonade bottles, framed suras from the Koran, carpets covering plastic seats the colour of ox blood. There are flowers on every table, even if they are plastic, and old men sit cross-legged on a raised platform, eating and debating. The pilau rice is full of raisins and beef, and almond and pistachio flakes have been sprinkled over the top. The men eat with their fingertips, placing the rice between their greasy lips. Experts, they interpret the rice in their own image: a good grain is straight, an old one has a bent back. The young Michael Douglas appears on the television screen, flies settling on him. People look away immediately.

'Would you like to have your stomachs ironed with some tea after the meal?'

Now men storm in from the street, tearing off their face masks. A fistful of long kebab skewers is thrown onto tin plates in front of them. They slide the pieces of meat off the skewer with a chunk of flat bread and an operatic gesture. The meat rolls onto the table between the artificial orange trees. The remaining half of the cow now has an almost glassy patina.

Nadia has five sisters and three brothers scattered around the world. So many microcosms, stories of adapting.

'Since I was a child I've known two worlds,' Nadia tells us. 'We celebrated days like New Year in a quite Western way, and we were allowed to play volleyball and swim in the pool. But we also had a guest house that women couldn't enter, and we wore the veil and enjoyed our freedoms largely between the walls of our house. Boys would look over our garden walls from neighbouring houses. We pretended not to notice.'

Nadia's family is from Kunduz, the city in the north that has been the focus of much fighting. Her father was the director of a cotton wool factory and a liberal man of some influence. Appreciative of the arts, he enabled his nine children to go to a good school and have a university education, a hidden liberal life. He let his own wife embark on all kinds of undertakings. Dressed as a young man, she was able to go to places that women normally never could.

When King Zahir Shah, while in Rome, was deposed in a coup by his cousin Daud, Nadia's father was thrown in prison without a trial for inciting rebellion. He was kept in solitary confinement as a 'political prisoner'. The family heard the news on the radio. That night Nadia, who was then the eldest in the house, slept with a revolver under her pillow. She secretly packed all her things and two days later fled to Kabul over the Salang Pass.

Soon after that she married, moved to Germany with her Afghan husband and had two children. She was only reunited with her father after he was released and could visit her in Germany. None of them returned to live in Afghanistan, but Nadia and others founded the Afghanischer Frauenverein (Afghan Women's Organization). Through it they support women's education – even during the war, send aid into the country over the Pakistani border, travel in disguise into the country themselves, sponsor programmes for schools and widows, and build wells and schools.

Her father's theatre was destroyed in the war. Her cousin Turab took on the management of the cinema. He's a life-loving, free-thinking man in his late forties, whose stomach plays up sometimes. We'll stay with him, at Nadia's family home in Kunduz.

His name alone is enough, already Nadia and Mirwais are telling the old stories – how he smashed an ink pot on his teacher's head, how he threw his sister's shoes into the stream so that they couldn't leave, how he pulled their burkas down. Today his eight siblings are all over the world. Only he and his sister have stayed. They couldn't go to their mother's funeral in the United States or to their brother's in Germany. He couldn't bear to leave Kunduz with his young wife and his two daughters. He lets his women, as he says, empty his pockets, but he's a kind-hearted man who only occasionally warns them, 'My pockets have eyes, you know.' But everyone knows that he's blind to what they see.

Another thing the war hasn't destroyed: goodwill.

'And your family? And back home? How are they?'

'Have a cup of tea! And please stay to eat! Please, do us the honour!'

A country that has had to cultivate both suspicion and compassion wouldn't let a temporary aberration like a war damage its culture.

I've learnt that when poor people ask if you'd like to eat, say no. If they had anything, it would already be on the table.

The immaterial things are what make cultures special, the gentle virtues and traditions that are most easily destroyed – for example, dignity and hospitality. How can such self-evident things be made evident to someone who doesn't know them?

~

We talk about the cinema in Kunduz.

'What if I give the women in Kunduz a free showing?'

'How would that work?'

'I buy a copy of a film, we announce a film just for women, and show it as a closed event. Men have to stay outside.'

Palpable excitement. That would mean that after 20 years the cinema would again be showing a film that women could go and see! The cinema wouldn't be a place for teenagers and men, it would be a cultured place, as it used to be ...

But Nadia warns us, 'The women won't be brave enough to come to the cinema on their own. It'll be made difficult for them. They won't dare.'

So what could we do to entice the women to come? 'If we could show a children's film at the same time ...' Nadia suggests.

A children's film. Then the mothers would bring their daughters, girls would bring their sisters ... But how are we going to find a children's film in Kabul? Chicken Street is the only street where the foreign businessmen, soldiers and staff of relief organizations and embassies go to find their souvenirs. It sells everything from carpets, lacquerwork, silver, lapis lazuli jewellery and little boxes, to old textiles or weapons, as well as postcards, CDs and DVDs.

That evening we phone her cousin Turab, the cinema's manager. For around £100 he gets a film for women. We can choose a film from his list. But we have to bring the children's film ourselves. It's fine if we bring a DVD.

So we go to Chicken Street and look for something appropriate. In the meantime Turab will look for the right projectors in Kunduz.

Nadia's parents had introduced a women's day to the cinema forty years ago. A little later their daughters even dared to sneak into the men's showings. The back rows were simply left free for them, and the girls squeezed in, hidden in the dark. This was daring at first, but in the wake of these little acts of subversion other freedoms established themselves in the Seventies.

Everything beautiful is wrung from the practical. Better to create a garden than to build a road? Of course. Then the road goes somewhere: to the garden.

Artificial beauty, a beauty without any sense of history, has certainly found its way to Afghanistan quickly: plastic flowers, oil print posters of Bollywood films and devotional articles for its stars. A plastic swan sits on a window ledge in our hotel, a dried flower stretches its stem indignantly out of its back and towards the curtains.

We leave the city and head for Paghman. Less than ten miles from Kabul, this little mountain resort for day trippers was where Nadia's family spent their summers. They came here for the two hottest months, enjoyed the cool breeze on the slopes, played volleyball, had parties, went to the town's theatre and cinema. On old pictures you can see relaxed holidaymakers in an ancient Afghanistan.

Nowadays bandits sometimes attack on the road to Paghman. So Mirwais calls on ahead before we set out, 'Is the road safe? Can we risk coming with our guests?'

He won't tell us who he's calling, but it must be someone who is closer to the gangs.

Paghman itself is a loose collection of huts, a few run-down stone buildings and a parade of vendors' stalls, over all of which towers a triumphal arch of French proportions. This freshly whitewashed monument is decorated with inscriptions and friezes commemorating the country's independence in 1919. It couldn't look more out of place than it does here, between a little monument with a stone flame, the bullet-scarred buildings, a fountain and flower beds which have been rolled out below it like a carpet in this post-war landscape.

The son of the family's gardener still lives nearby. His house is up a little mountain path where you have to tread carefully because of the mines. He has seen and survived everything and lives in a well-protected property. It sits above the plain, encircled by magnificently blooming potted plants and terraced flower beds. He often had to defend himself up here. He fortified his house and cropped his dog's ears to make it wilder. The dog jerks hard on his leash under the tree as we walk up. In the yard we see a container that says 'Humanitarian'. It's full of rubbish.

Only the weed covered garden is left of the home that used to bring a flood of holiday feelings to the family. The gardener's son's house, on the other hand, is the same as it ever was, its solid mud bricks stamped firmly into the slope. There was a time when he defended it with a shotgun, but he had to give up 'because of the women'. The fear was too strong that the approaching Russians could rape them. So the men packed up their goods and left with their families for a guerrilla war in the mountains, then to Pakistan where they re-organized, '... and then we beat the Russians'.

The old refrain. So then he returned, cleared out the attic to make room for storing firewood, and made the house home to the nine members of his family. He looks defensively down towards the town, and his melancholy teenage son also says he'd like to stay here, not to move down into the smoky town, among all those people. 'This is my land, my home, what I'll inherit, where else should I be?'

We're sitting in a circle on colourful cushions. Above us hang pictures of sunflowers and political posters that nobody can get passionate about. Light seeps through the narrow milky panes of glass into a room that is a threshing floor where carpets cover the bare earth floor, however much it would like to be a lounge.

By now the old man, who Nadia only knows as the gardener's son, is a person of authority himself. All day people come who want his advice. He arbitrates and counsels like a judge. He'd rather have sent his son, the dreamer, to university, 'but I didn't have enough money for the bribes'. So when the boy started to laze about with his school-leaving certificate in hand, his father made him the teacher without further ado. Now he teaches the small children and it's planned that he'll run the whole school later.

Decisions have to be made by those with knowledge and authority, not with the right qualifications, things are too urgent. Last year there were 30 children lumped together in one class. Now there are seven classes, each of 40 children, most of whom have returned from Pakistani refugee camps. They learn religion, reading and writing, mathematics, drawing and sport, but they've brought a different language, different gestures and different clothes back with them, as well as different sports and ideals. At least a black school uniform has now been devised which, in contrast to the brown one-piece shirt and trousers from Pakistan, is a real suit and evokes no unpleasant memories.

I ask the student teacher, 'Do you have a wife?'

He smiles resignedly, 'You're asking a terrible question. Where should I get enough money for a wife? Where?'

'Life's corpse has no burial cloth,' the father adds, a metaphor for poverty, but a metaphor that resonates beyond the poverty here.

~

The next meal awaits us after nightfall at Khaled's. We're driving in two cars; he overtakes and steers our little convoy to his house, as if it were the most natural thing in the world. Who's going to object?

His inconspicuous terraced house looks as if it would be home to a small nuclear family. But we pass a whole phalanx of burkas on the coat hooks. Brightly-dressed young women also flit through the house. We won't get a better look at any of them, however much we or they might wish it. The driver and head of the house sets the rules here, and they are stricter than those that Nadia knew and negotiated.

It's strange to come to know a country without any female faces. You could get delirious thinking about what's missing, make it up, transpose it into the realm of fairy tales, hallucinate any number of old-fashioned physiognomies. What do these colourful hazes leave you with? Scents, wide open eyes between eyeliner, quarter profiles, all blurred as they turn away and flee.

The guest room is under the many, protective arms of a gigantic chandelier, in which a single bulb is burning. A boy accompanies me to the washroom in the basement. He shoos the girls out of the way first, but they still whip around on the threshold. Watchful as fox cubs. When we go upstairs again the room where the girls had been is silent.

'How many people live in this house?'

'Umm, 18,' replies Khaled. 'No, 19.' Later he says, '21', adding in a vexed tone: 'It's because of the children. You never really know how many there are at any one time.' Then he laughs and says, 'But three more or less doesn't change things much!'

Rice dishes, meat in a sauce, kebabs, all brought in by almost invisible forces. When there's a power cut no one comments on it. Three men just flip open their mobile phones and people eat in the cold blue pool of light their displays throw. Then two gas lamps are brought. The conversation doesn't stop.

'... my older brother fought for 19 years as a soldier. After he got injured, his right leg was three centimetres shorter. He became a pharmacist. Now he's been laid off. There's no pension, the state is broke. So how are you supposed to live? And be happy?'

People look around the circle. No one moves. The faces show a stubborn pride, embarrassment, courage, and anger too.

'I didn't even register to vote.'

'We're angry because the old commanders are back in power. The UN Commission for Human Rights said that no one should be in the elections who has blood on their hands. And now? There they sit! Let me tell you, I fled to Pakistan and stayed there with my wife and children for a whole 13 years. Now we come back, and there they are again! The UN has turned a blind eye to the drugs. The opium fields start right at Kabul's city limits! And in the north our drugs inspectors are still on bicycles!'

The news is just being read on television that four escaped prisoners from Bagram detention centre have been re-captured. It took time for me to learn to equate this camp that people barely spoke about in Europe with Guantanamo. People are tortured here, prisoners die here, many others are sent on to Kandahar or Guantanamo. Looking at the television pictures of American soldiers proud to have brought the prisoners back, everyone in the room goes silent.

'None of them are interested in having a strong government here, least of all the US.'

'And corruption is so entrenched that it really should be in the constitution.'

'Do you know this one?' one of them exclaims. 'Bush and Karzai meet. Bush says, you have to get rid of corruption. Good, replies Karzai, I'll get rid of it. What'll you give me if I do?'

His listeners don't laugh, they smile. 'It's not my best joke,' he apologizes.

Mirwais brings up the road tolls that every Tom, Dick and Harry demands. When goods finally arrive, they are either only a fraction of what was sent or are prohibitively expensive.

'So why did you vote for Karzai in the presidential elections?'

'Because he was the least of the evils. And because his father fought in the resistance.'

A pause. Then Khaled says abruptly, 'I'm sorry that I'm so quiet today, my uncle died yesterday.'

Someone asks what he died of.

'What he died of? He died of grief at what has become of our country.'

The turbaned old man in the corner listens attentively, commenting at the most with a facial gesture. He was a taxi driver in Kabul for 37 years. Before that he was a driver for the royal family, and so when he does speak he says with conviction that the Afghans would have been best off with the King to hold together all the tribes and institutions. People could agree on him. But the US foiled that.

The King is wheelchair-bound. He's very well advanced in years, speaks slowly and has little impact. He still inspects military parades though, to keep up appearances. A number of people in the room voice agreement.

'Yes, the King is the father of the nation!'

'Just the King!'

Everyone, of every age, seems to know something about politics. In addition, the old taxi driver knows the stories that all taxi drivers know.

'Have children been born in your taxi?' I ask.

'Have they ever! And I've delivered a child all on my own, because there wasn't a midwife there.'

'Have people died in your taxi?'

'Sometimes during the war injured people were put in my taxi, even ones in comas. Yes, some of them didn't wake up again.'

'And have you ever caused an accident?'

He chooses a full legal sentence for his reply. 'In 37 years I have not once so much as brushed someone's clothing.'

'And you?' I ask the off-duty policeman. 'Do you stick to the traffic rules?'

He laughs diplomatically. 'I take advantage of my uniform.'

Then Mirwais lifts a finger to silence us. 'I have to see this!'

For a second time everyone turns to the television. A sketch is on. Everyone starts laughing before much has happened. It turns out it's a scene of Boccaccian humour. A mother and daughter go to an old doctor. It's the mother who needs to see him, but the doctor only has eyes for her daughter and gives her a thorough examination, while he leaves the mother in pain. Everyone laughs. In the best sequence, the doctor has the mother, then the daughter say 'ah'. It becomes a canon that the three sing. At the end it becomes clear that the doctor wasn't a doctor after all, just the night watchman. Now everyone's laughing in sudden glee, a laughter of complete innocence.

We turn over to the ministers' parade. Everyone gesticulates at the television. 'Look, the defence minister! The most corrupt of them all! Half of Kabul belongs to him!'

Then we see the health minister distributing money in envelopes as he goes from bed to bed in a hospital.

'Why the envelopes?'

'Because it's so little money.'

Then the energy minister, who says, 'I'm proud that there's electricity.'

Hoots of laughter. 'We have an electricity pole right outside, just not the electricity. He's clever – everyone who's watching television has electricity too, but most get it from a generator. That's the truth, not that he'll let on.'

Everyone has a word to add to the decades' long routine of distrusting politicians. I ask what power the defence ministry has.

'Huh! The US broke it too. Everyone that was in military training was dismissed. We're helpless if there's any catastrophe, fire or earthquake! Where's our pride? What's different about us? OK, we don't say "terrorist activity" on television, we say "destructive activity". That's a start, we leave the other word to the Americans.'

Again it falls to Mirwais to bring the discussion to a close. He does so with the biblical gravity of Job: 'God loves us, that's why he burdens us with so many problems.'

'When I decline an invitation in Germany,' Nadia says, 'I just have to say that I have a project. In Afghanistan I say I have guests.'

The hippy trail is also our own, rather unloved past. Do we want to see ourselves or our parents like that, searchers in fur coats and clouds of smoke for mind-expanding, self-transcending experience?

Western youth fell into this country with little understanding for the nature of its liberality. They too were colonialists, here to compensate for the afflictions of their societies and seldom questioning what their idea of freedom meant for a country that had learnt to think differently about how tradition and new ways relate.

The fact that drugs were available and not illegal did not make the Afghan society of the Sixties and Seventies a realm ruled and lived in according to hippy ideals. They found themselves in a country that they didn't understand and that didn't understand them, and became dropouts, tramps, bag ladies or big spenders, but without any dignity. Some stayed. Ghosts of their past dreams, they still hang around at some drug trafficking backwater, bearded, bedraggled and addicted. I met one at a checkpoint on a road near the Oxus. He tottered against a railing, gazing wanly out into the landscape and murmuring to himself like a Sufi.

Europeans and Americans have a way of being friendly and chummy as if the distances between people always seem too big to them. They like to be hearty, warm.

There they stand, in this foreign place, and find the people around them even more foreign, even more lost to the world, and, after all the years of wars, invasions and interventions, even more suspicious than they had expected.

And yet the Afghans show an openness that isn't present in the West. Not out of need, or to curry favours. Rather a respect for the other person's undamaged nature brings them closer together. A warmth like an underlying feeling of goodwill. It's linked to the sense that when you first arrive in a country, you are better able to get a feeling for it, than to know about it.

We go to Chicken Street on the hunt for a short film that children can watch and which doesn't have too much English, so that people can follow it. In the end we leave the shop with a Laurel and Hardy collection from which we can choose a suitable half-hour film that evening. Nadia will have to use a microphone to read the titles between shots for everyone in the room. That could work. Yet it's still strange to think how a Laurel and Hardy film would change if you saw it through the eyes of an Afghan child. Stan Laurel as a woman – is that all right? He lies on the tracks – will that be understood, are we expecting too much? Will they realize that the slapstick violence is not real?

The small boy Christian to whom I had given a piece of chocolate that morning is waiting on the road in the evening. 'Hey, mister,' he shouts in English. 'Where is my chocolate?'

At night we are under house arrest. Before dark the side roads are too dangerous, after dark all roads are. The power cuts out so often that it is impossible to read. We move around in the dark, we hear a scurrying through the garden, then the generator kicks in again.

In the morning a soldier gets up from the flower bed, takes a drink from the garden hose, shoulders his Kalashnikov and continues his patrol. The new day climbs over the mud roofs, through a haze that gives everything a pastel hue.

We head north out of town towards Kunduz. 'If the heart is big, the smallest space is enough,' say the Afghans. Because there are six of us in the car, Mirwais squeezes in between our luggage. He squats there for hours, almost invisibly, becoming a warrior once more.

We pass the Asia Wedding Hall, one of the new facilities catering for people with limited space at home. Here they can celebrate, with men and women in separate rooms. Then comes the Top World Gym with its hand painted Arnold Schwarzenegger, whose chest seems even more grotesquely unnatural here than it does normally.

Then a line of Pakistani-style buildings whose façades are painted with patterns like those on carpets, and which are decorated with battlements, coloured tiles and columns. Then the market stalls where furry car-seat covers, exhausts and bicycle inner tubes hang on crossbeams. The stallholders wear combat gear.

The destruction seems less intense on the mountain slopes. Mud brick cubes teeter on the edge of deep chasms. The next earthquake – and the last one in Pakistan could be felt here too – or the next rock fall could pull everything down with it. Exposed to all this shaking and sliding, and avalanches too, mines move and even cleared fields become risky again.

Water is the biggest problem. Every litre has to be dragged up from the valley. Each settlement is beige or ochre, the air is dusty and cold. Massud's broodingly melancholic face is painted on façades everywhere, as well as in the landscape and at roadsides. With his drooping eyelids he looks like a poet, not a military commander.

Like no other person in recent Afghan history, this charismatic man lends himself to idolization. But didn't he make common cause with the Russians? When his troops reached Kabul didn't they just plunder and rape like other bands of irregulars? Wasn't he really just, as Mirwais says, 'one commander among many'?

~

There was a time when women didn't drink anything before setting out for Kunduz, because there were scarcely any opportunities for them to go to the toilet on the way. Now mines are the greatest danger for anyone who leaves the road.

We drive into a barren landscape. With their chimneys and encircling walls the brickworks in the plains look like old temples. Their high smokestacks make them visible from far off. Day labourers go to these Pakistani-run factories to slave away for a pittance. Instead of a desert plain, vineyards once stretched out here. People said it was the greenest place in the region.

Destruction was visited on both nature and people here, quite intentionally. The Taliban eradicated the Tajiks outright from this area. Anyone who survived, fled to Pakistan. Infertile fields and dilapidated irrigation systems were left. Today it's hard to see anything but destruction in this valley – fields becoming wilderness, broken down walls, the pink ruins of houses and the colourful bundles of flags at roadside martyrs' graves. The air is becoming clearer.

'Just wait, wine will come back.'

~

Soviet tanks can still be seen everywhere, and are still in use.

Sometimes a homeless person uses one to doss down in, or their metal parts are turned into tin cans. Some of them look like the focus of archaeological excavations. The children investigate and dismantle them. They acquire technical knowledge. Even the sale of small batteries was banned under the Taliban. They could have been used in walkie-talkies. Nowadays children are fascinated by everything that can be made to jump, shine or shoot with electricity.

~

Children sit under the shelters that stand in for a market, watching over scarce supplies of fruit. There's only an abundance of grapes, their small berries come in a wide variety of colours. Next to them are piles of potatoes, eggs, biscuits, red onions, pepperoni, radishes, mandarins, salted nuts, melons, small bananas and crackers.

Yet meat is at the centre of it all. Between the butchers' stalls where stallholders still lug halves of animals over their shoulders, a carousel clatters. A wheel on a pole holds three wooden berths in which children fly round and round, as a man keeps pushing them. Right next to them a calf is just being slaughtered in an open space between stands. Buying meat is a man's job, and men can also spend a whole evening discussing what is the best rice and how to prepare it.

Its fore and hind legs lashed together, the calf is wrestled down and its neck pressed to the dusty ground. As the butcher draws his broad-bladed knife across its throat with a conductor's flourish, the animal's eyes bulge. At first it looks as though something in the distance demands its full attention, then as if its eyes want to tear themselves out of their sockets. Apart from that it doesn't move at all. Only the tail tuft keeps beating rhythmically and insistently on the ground where it has woven itself in amongst the onlookers' legs. Then suddenly its legs start to flee, twitching first, then running, lengthy strides turning to scurrying. Its head rises too, as if it wanted to stretch the neck, upwards, and its eyes peer at distant sights, upwards.

Then a sigh, then the sobbing death-rattle. Its agony lasts a long time. The calf lowers its head to the ground, right above a channel into which its blood is now gushing thickly. Its tail slows down, its gaze lowers to the mirror of its own blood. That's where it finally rests, all pathos extinguished.

The faces around ask if there's still life in its body. The calf looks at its death very matter-of-factly. The onlookers are quite silent. Nobody laughs. There's something symbolic in every death.

'The best meat is the meat that doesn't have any death in it,' says Khaled. But can you eat any meat without also eating the animal's fear at death?

They will eat and use almost everything from this carcass. The metamorphosis of a living creature into food has begun, and there will be some meat for the beggars. A man scuttles over who spent days trekking to Kabul across the mountains. He didn't take food for the journey with him, I ask him why.

'Whoever comes from the mountains doesn't need provisions. The route down is fertile.'

In the meantime the carousel has reached its top speed. An old man keeps reaching between the rods and giving it another push. The children's faces are a blur, no one's screaming. The ride is fun, and a kind of test. Music starts up from a transistor radio at the top of a pile of tyres, no bass, just tinny high notes. Romantic slush: our world music.

In the meantime the men have already cut the calf into two warm halves. One half lies in the dust, the other doesn't hang well, a hook tears into its flesh until its twisted head comes to rest in the dirt, its gaping neck wound stretched out accusingly at the onlookers.

Two men arrive, kissing each other in greeting between the dripping halves of the carcass. The next lot of children yells on the carousel, the radio blares out Bollywood music now, and a group of youngsters have set up a game of hoopla on the ground. Whoever wins can take a ladleful of soup from the pot they're sitting around.

So this is a holiday morning on an Afghan country road. Its archaic, ceremonial, brave, innocent, childish and pragmatic elements are all interwoven, and shared among all age groups. The mix is so different than in our world. The norms and mores are almost unimaginably foreign to us, and yet the scene and the ways it interprets life are full of magic.

A bearded fighter roars up on a moped, carrying a giant cuddly lion on his pillion seat. The driver almost disappears in the animal's woolly fur. Its paws stretch around him from behind. He brakes to examine the freshly slaughtered animal. The children get off the carousel and crowd around him. A little girl shakes hands with the lion. The rough man puts his foot on the gas again and drives off towards the Hindu Kush with his cuddly lion.

'That's just the photographer,' says an Afghan doctor who doesn't enjoy the same attention. 'He travels from fair to fair with his prop.'

I ask the doctor, who specializes in ear, nose and throat, what sort of a life he can look forward to now. He's well educated, and respiratory diseases are common ailments in this smoggy area.

'We looked forward to peace for 30 years,' he says with a shrug. 'Now we don't know what it is and what to do with it.'

'But you survived!'

'Yes, and I wore my blood on the palm of my hand!' – The Afghan expression meaning 'I was in mortal danger'.

The settlements on the plain lie there like low-lying castles. Everything has been wrestled from nature here, everything has to defend itself from the war and be both inconspicuous and defendable. Sometimes the monotony is so oppressive that flowers and fruit seem to scream, like over-exaggerated artificial effects.

I ask a young nomad boy, 'Why do you have a green mark at the root of your nose?'

'So that people can find me again.'

'And where do you think that I come from?'

'From China.'

He wants to know why I am here.

'No reason,' I say. 'I'm just travelling.'

He turns to his friend and says, 'Look, our first tourist.'

A girl at the street market invites us to come to her house for a cup of tea.

'But what will your mother say?'

'My mother is dead.'

We decline, explaining how far we still have to travel. The girl gives me an egg for the journey. If I were to give her something now, I'd spoil her generous gesture. In a cultural sphere like our own where everything is based on exchange, it takes practice to receive things with the right gesture, words and actions.

Love songs are blaring from the car radio too. Their lyrics span the breadth of lovers' talk, from 'You are married, but I still love you' to 'Darling, come on and give me the balm for my sore tooth'. A melody soars to the heights of a male falsetto voice, while at the wheel Khaled is telling such funny stories that Nadia teases him, saying it sounds as though he had swallowed two radios.

6

All the places we drive through have names that hark back to the past. One refers to a freedom fighter who fought the British, another one to a ruler who only held power for nine months and was illiterate, but wise, another to a courageous mujaheddin. Some houses carry the English inscription 'Cleared' – of fighters, mines or inhabitants?

One village is called 'Massacre'. Its inhabitants opposed the Russians. The men went to fight. All 700 women and children were killed in the village by Soviet soldiers. When the men returned they found their village had become a memorial to a massacre. They decided to stay, and still live in Massacre today.

German relief projects can be identified from a distance by the traffic signs that precede them. One, for example, warns that pedestrians cross the road here. What is an Afghan to think of this? Pedestrians cross these roads everywhere. The sign shows a girl with her plaits bobbing behind her. They are the first I've seen in all Afghanistan. Are Afghan women to think: Careful! German Heidis cross the road here?

Instead of Heidis, a line of skinned cows is carried across the road. No sign warned us of them but the lanes are sprinkled with their blood.

~

The rivers flow cold and green from the nearest mountains of the Hindu Kush. It rises above us, a muddy yellow, then a rocky grey, then covered in snow. Butchers' stalls line the roads in these Arcadian high plateaus. Fruit sellers come from far away to settle the narrow strips where the rivers have washed up a few yards of fertile earth, and where fruit and nuts grow. Their houses are often on the bare mountainsides higher up. But today they have brought their children with them for the three days of Eid. They're wearing festive clothing, embroidered little dresses with colourful hems and silk decoration, and thick pullovers and jackets. Just one of these children stepping out of the door of a mud hut is a feast of colour in this landscape.

So in a little shop I buy an old, richly embroidered child's waistcoat that was made in Central Afghanistan in the Forties. The borders round the collar and down its front are embroidered in blue on the orange cloth. Little round mirrors have been set into the decorations and animals that are sewn onto it. Flowers and birds cover the hems in colourful opulence, each pattern is new and the workmanship is of such fine and detailed quality that this piece of clothing can absorb your attention for a long time, including its threadbare patches and little stains. They have to stay. Hard to imagine what child walked around in this waistcoat, as splendidly dressed as an Indian prince or a South American princess.

7

On a hillside a tank graveyard with at least a hundred burnt-out, dismantled and stripped tanks, guarded round the clock. Why? They're to form the basis of a museum. Why? You still can't imagine a generation in this country that needs to see a hundred destroyed tanks to remember what war is.

The rocks' outlines and contours are becoming more pronounced, gullies appear, the air suddenly smells of mountains, and the water too. Two young men walk hand-in-hand to a defensive wall, where they sit down on a small open patch of grass to have a picnic. They have brought flat bread and almonds. Looking around, there's nothing in sight that couldn't have been exactly the same a thousand years ago. Even the almonds are surrounded by stories. I think of Nadia's stories and of the melancholy words of another exile, Saira Shah's father, who said 'I've given you stories that replace a people. They are your people.'

Out here too, on the road over the Salang Pass, many houses are missing their roofs and have bullet holes in their walls. Here too the weapons of war have become part of the reconstructed houses: a ledge made of sawn-off mortar shells, a windowsill decorated with spent cartridges.

The river fans out in the valley. The homesteads sit like castles against the mountainsides, high-walled family farms clawing into the rocks. No outsiders will stay here. The families intermarry: we pass some strange-looking children.

Tiny footpaths lead over the mountain ridges and down to a place where a makeshift bridge – just a tank track thrown over three steel girders – provides access to the road.

The houses are perhaps 200 or 300 feet above the roaring water that allows fruit and nut trees to be planted in the loops and spits of land. Travellers stop here in the summer to spread out a blanket, wash their feet in the cold water and eat mulberries. They can transform the most barren places into groves for their uncomplicated pleasures.

Mirwais warns again and again, 'You stick out a mile away, watch out! Don't walk around alone!'

In this idyllic setting we forget about danger. He always looks worried. He alone carries the responsibility for our safety, no one else, least of all Nadia or me.

We never know what's making him worried, whether there's an urgent reason for it or his thoughts are somewhere ahead of us. Emergencies are banal. A country road lay bathed in sunlight. A moment later it lies there just the same, but smoke is pouring from a wrecked car, bodies lie in the ditch.

And even with just 'simple ambushes' and spontaneous muggings, it's impossible to know when and why it escalates, and to what extent.

Perhaps the highwayman's job is inspired by the landscape around us. The men here know only this landscape, and thanks to it have survived in it. How could they not make use of the only knowledge that gives them an advantage over others?

~

We wind our way up mountainsides to the 10,000-foot high Salang Tunnel. No wonder that no settlements can be seen from the air. The villages up here are like collections of boxes piled together on top of each other in basic cubic forms.

From outside it's scarcely possible to see how these complexes fit together inside. Far below it looks like cattle are grazing at the river's edge. Where will people descend to herd them? We can't guess. Gatherers of homeopathic herbs descend into the valley too, as well as children looking for wood; even a burka on high heels has wandered here by mistake. Wolves, jackals and leopards pad along here too.

Once Himalayan cedar, spruce, pine, larch, oak and birch trees grew on these slopes. Yet most have been cleared now. Hazelnut, pistachio, walnut and mulberry trees are still planted in the narrow valleys though, and grow alongside apricot, peach, apple and pear trees, as well as roses, honeysuckle, hawthorn, irises and tulips.

Mirwais doesn't only know this landscape from having driven through it so often. He survived the war in these mountains. He would cross their ridges, because the Salang Pass was too dangerous or was closed. He crossed minefields, lived off mulberries and sometimes brought bread from far away to sell in the high villages. Women, children and refugees often made a living like this. On the other side of the ridge you could again travel by car. But entering another tribe's territory you would get into a car from that territory. That was safer.

And then suddenly at the side of the road we come across a grove, a stream, fruit trees and patches of open meadow. There are carved birds in the water and scrapped tanks polished so smoothly that many children's bottoms must have slid over them.

There is a little wall there too and a lean-to, where a prayer mat can be spread out, and then gradually, like ghosts, bowls appear with grapes and almonds, dried peas, pistachios and fresh water. Where from? It all comes from up there, where the old General sits in his house. He set this place up and built the mosque, so creating work for a good number of people in the area.

"You have to visit him! You should at least visit him on your way back!"

The apples are bursting with juice. Every piece of fruit that comes from here has been wrung from the earth, every tree has strained to push its sap into its branches and twigs and has pressed a clear juice into the blossoms, leaves and then the pulp of the fruit. Even their sweetness seems to have been squeezed out of the state of emergency and suffering in which they grew.

Zalmai, a young boy who is the former General's emissary here, juggles the trays of food. He's in charge of goats, chickens and sheep up there, of apple, walnut and plum trees, and he has to go to school. There he sits in a class of 50 children, many older than he is, and learns Dari, maths, algebra, geography and geometry.

Older boys are in his class because they have returned from the war. When they want to explain the difference between anti-personnel mines and anti-tank mines to Zalmai, he waves away the explanation. 'I've seen them myself lots of times.' The boy holds his open palm upwards, like an old man would.

Winter here is hard and long. Only three in every hundred families have a television.

'And you?'

'We tell each other stories, or read them out, we play chess.'

He leaves, excusing himself. His kite is stuck in trees, he has to get it down.

He won't have noticed this himself, but everything that Zalmai said, he said with a knitted brow.

'Salaam alaikum,' I say as he goes.

'Good boy,' he replies in English.

~

When Nadia wants to remember something, she writes it in Persian on her palm as she did at school. It's as if even this action is a return.

And then all these places, each with their stories: Istalef, where turquoise pots are made, Charikar, the valley of fruit trees and vineyards, which today are withered after years of drought. We are on the old caravanserai routes over the Hindu Kush. We'll make it to their end in seven hours, if all the bridges are intact, if we don't have to cross raging white waters, if the Salang Pass is open.

And then we drive into the Salang Tunnel, the infamous tube at either end of which the mujaheddin fought against the Russians, and the Northern Alliance against the Taliban, and mercenaries against bands of irregulars. It's the most heavily mined stretch. Nadia winds her window down. 'You have to stick your head out and shout: Salang, my dear, I'll come back! The echo will be amazing.'

A dark wall of rock sheers upwards in front of the bunker-like tunnel. On its steep surface someone has written 'Be Happy!' And we're happy as we drive into the tunnel's mouth. During the war it was impassable, either blocked or mined, and after the war it was closed off with cables.

Again and again we hit a pitch black stretch. In between pale blocks of light fall through air holes, along with flurries of snowflakes that blow into the tunnel like confetti. There's no electric lighting or ventilation. We keep finding big round patches of ice covering the asphalt. The walls are varnished with ice too wherever water has dripped in through damaged sections. We drive further and further up in a carefully snaking line.

Arriving on the other side, Mirwais says, 'A warm welcome to northern Afghanistan.'

Silence. It's the harsher, colder and less hospitable side of the pass, the region where he once fought, the area that people wanted to partition off and where resistance was strong. Today the first thing we see are the ruins of the road workers' little settlements. Once the workers had finished one section of the road, they would take the roofs off their huts and drag the valuable wood down to where they next settled. There they would immediately set up a tent school for their children. You can't find anyone here who doesn't defend the value of literacy and education.

These are regions where nature eradicates life. People's response is colour, and sometimes even cotton will bloom. It's a landscape which for most of its expanse appears to be 'nothing': stone, earth, bulk, texture, structure. And then something tiny stands out like a red dot in one of Corot's paintings: a headscarf, the spot of a cow, a nomad child in bright clothing. Just a single thing, it moves through the monochrome landscape as an embodiment of the Afghan injunction to 'shoulder yourself'.

I ask Mirwais about a lavishly-decorated grave right by a steep drop.

'It's the Cleaner's grave.'

The 'Cleaner' rode beside bus drivers, cleared the road when need be, and helped with luggage. Once a bus slipped back, rolling towards the drop beyond the road. The Cleaner jumped out to look for something to put behind the wheels. Not finding anything, he lay down behind the back wheels and was killed, saving 52 passengers.

'Those were the days,' says Mirwais. 'Nobody would do that nowadays.'

The grave is fenced in and adorned with red and green pennants. The wind has worn the little flags threadbare. From a distance this resting place looks like a luxuriant flowering bush on the rock.

The plain opens out, the road descends. The stalls we pass now are hung with a delicious fish caught in the mountain streams. People come a long way for it. Yet as each area is above all known for its own speciality fruit, this area is called 'Melon Valley'.

On the mined slope a nomad has put up his wide low tent – a half-nomad in fact, spending his summers here and his winters in Jalalabad. Nomads like him are Afghanistan's true forefathers, their pitching camp and moving on have altered the country's tribes and landscapes.

Then a few unkempt boys with donkeys come along, then camels with their teenage herdsmen. Goats climb rashly over the rocks and below, where the plain slopes downwards, the rice terraces have been walled in and given underground irrigation.

Shepherds drive their lean sheep through the pastel-coloured fields where farmers sit and inspect the rice and wheat that are harvested twice a year. As most of them live on hilltops or on the higher, more protected slopes, they have their sons fetch water in canisters. About 15 times a day they have to make the mile-long journey to the river and back again. Two are coming back now, chatting affably under their burdens.

Looking out over the plain from the vantage point of a high boulder, you spy an idyllic scene. Horses, cows and camels roam freely, men and women, mostly dressed in white, walk in little groups, children clown around, and healthy stems of rice shoot up from puddles of water.

The ridges on the far side of the valley are ochre in the mist. The valley seems to be brimful of birdsong and dogs' barking, and sometimes a child, a horn, the lowing of a cow – as if everything had been composed to be in harmony. The Ismailis have settled in the wide river valleys around here. Today many followers of this branch of Islam live in Pakistan and India. In Afghanistan they have made this valley their own and given it a truly Arcadian aspect.

A man in the middle of the field prays facing Mecca. Behind his back two grotesque turkeys are pecking in the same direction.

How far a little girl like the one here, driving a sheep before her, has to travel if she wants to get to the world, to any world, such as the one she supposes we inhabit. We are wrapped in the foreignness that is part of her yearning. We smell of it, we breathe it out. We are the winners who are just passing through, people who can't be observed because we travel in a different element: transitoriness.

The next stop is Little Moscow. The roadblocks are made of tank tracks and Soviet military equipment has been used in the foundations of the shacks, while the rivers wash up more scrap from the war.

In places like these we may perhaps mention that the Communists fought illiteracy, gave women more rights and gave labourers in the factories and fields a consciousness of their position. It's said that many intellectuals live here. Translated, that means many followers of a partially sensible, outdated, impractical and, above all, non-Afghan outlook.

Often men are just squatting at the side of the road, looking for hours in one direction, and then the other.

We feel their eyes on us. They watch us until we have disappeared. The way we act isn't plausible, and an unveiled Nadia attracts more stares here than a white foreigner. It's not clear what we want, why we have stopped and walk first this and then that way. We're observed with uninterested goodwill, a little sceptically too.

In fact all we're looking for at this country market is bolani, our turnovers filled with spicy potatoes. But because a crush of onlookers starts to develop, all teenage ex-soldiers, and because Mirwais starts to worry about our safety, we have to leave. The grown men are looking displeased too. Some of them, not without envy, see us less for what we do than for where we can return to.

Nadia tells us about the Kunduz of her childhood, their games and dances, picnics in the flowering steppe, nearby excavations of Buddhist relics. Only when she gets to the horse-drawn carriages, mentioning their red-lined seats, the plumes on the horses' heads and the sound of bells in the streets, does she have to stop and turn her overflowing eyes away to the hills, helpless before her own past as only those can be who have had theirs taken away.

Nadia tells us about the cinema in Kunduz too. Once it was her world. An old theatre with a balcony and a wide Cinemascope screen, it survived the war. It could seat 400 people.

'Don't expect too much. It's old and run-down. It's suffered.'

Years ago the Taliban wanted to close this cinema completely too. Turab, a skilled manager, offered them a compromise: half cinema, half clinic. So the projection room was closed and declared a clinic. Yet as the Taliban really wanted to make the whole cinema part of their mosque, they called again and asked Turab a cunning question, 'What would you like to have, a cinema or a mosque?'

'Both.'

The next day he was sent for, but he sent someone on his behalf, just to be safe. That person reported back that big sticks were propped up and waiting in a corner. The same evening Turab fled to Kabul in a rickety aeroplane.

Khaled, who has been listening from the driver's seat, asks me not without ulterior motive, 'And you? Would you chose a mosque or a cinema?'

'Both.'

'Equally?'

'Both mould people.'

He thinks for a minute. It's the 'Render unto Caesar that which is Caesar's' answer. Then he says, 'True. We learnt in the cinema how to wage war, how to lay explosives, things like that …'

The storm passes.

~

As long ago as the 1930s, Robert Byron wrote that Afghans liked to say that travelling to Kunduz is practically suicide. Others said 'you go to Kunduz to die'. They said this because of its bogs, mosquitoes, scorpions and snakes.

Later the Indian film star Feroz Khan filmed on the steppe here, and Omar Sharif and Jack Palance starred in *The Horsemen*. In their wake a few European celebrities and crowned heads turned up, and so the slogan was soon coined 'Live a little, come to Kunduz'.

Today battered old Kunduz seems to be gathering itself, waking up, but it also points to the past with its camels, horse-drawn carriages, old stables, and the separate market areas for spices, textiles, dried fruits and meat. The war has left its traces in the town, and yet old façades are still intact. The

Spinzar cotton wool factory, which Nadia's father had run, is still there. Old trees stand in the courtyards. There's a colonial feel in the air.

Yet the childhood courtyard where Nadia grew up both free and sheltered is bare and dilapidated. There are still a few bushes and flower beds, but the swimming pool is full of earth and rubble, the trees have been cut down, only the façade and its small veranda and semicircle of staircase seem the same. This is where fluffy pillows and mattresses were laid out on hot summer nights. The girls would drink tea spiced with cardamom and look at the night sky, while the aunts told love stories about Layla and Majnun, another episode every night.

Nadia's school for girls was right beside a religious school. The high walls around liberal family life almost touched the high walls of the Islamic institute. None of the walls was high enough.

'We always made fun of their parrot talk,' says Nadia of the Koranic students, 'because they always repeat everything. Once one of us even dared to creep into their library and studied a sex education book there. So little by little we were educated according to the book.'

'Are you sure you know it all correctly now?'

In the evening we go over from the guesthouse, where we men will sleep, to the main house, which has rooms for women and children. Every evening a banquet is held in its lounge with its red plastic chairs under crossed halberds and a photo of a German wood.

Turab's wife is in her ninth month. She shows herself, but eats in the kitchen. The other women stay in the back rooms. Mirwais, Khaled, another employee, cousins and distant relations are almost always there. Others make visits. We eat the most delicious pilau rice with the straightest of grains. It accompanies ragout, shish kebabs, chickpeas and eggs.

'This egg is from a Taliban hen,' someone says.

'What are Taliban hens?'

'The ones that run around freely.'

Then colourful jelly puddings, blancmanges that taste of rosewater, pale biscuits.

Nadia tells of their journeys into the steppe, when they travelled north to the Oxus, the legendary river on Afghanistan's northern border.

'Father stood at the river, which borders Turkmenistan, Tajikistan and Uzbekistan, and said the Russians would come sometime.'

'They told us that in Germany too,' I reply.

'But they really did come here.'

We're talking about the film.

'Don't expect too much,' says Turab, who knows his cinema. 'Reckon with 13 people, maybe less.'

'It's free,' protests Mirwais. 'It'll be bursting at the seams.'

But how are the right people to hear about our film? By word of mouth.

'I'll go out and tell the women about it,' says Nadia. 'We used to do it with a horse and carriage, posters and a drum. But we don't have that now.'

So we move with the times: we need a television ad on the local Kunduz channel. The others draft a text in Dari and then translate it for me: 'A German humanist and friend of Afghanistan …'

'Wait,' says Turab. 'You need to put 'Free' at the start.'

'Does it have to be a humanist and friend of Afghanistan?'

'We can't use your name. Names are too dangerous!'

'Then his profession!'

'But then they'll immediately want to kidnap him.'

'But – humanist?'

'That works, no one understands it.'

'OK, so: "Free! A German humanist and friend of Afghanistan invites all Kunduz's women and children to see a children's film and an Indian film at 2 p.m." And then we'll add "Free" again,' Turab decides, before adding after a pause, 'I'm guessing 13 people.'

Nadia imagines a whole army of women who're awaiting liberation and so are bound to come. Moreover, they're going to find out about it very quickly as she'll tell them all in person.

Discussion turns to the projector, which has to be fetched from a distant province, and to the choice of the 'woman's film'. Nadia and I are for a schmaltzy Bollywood film with sugary sweet music, exuberant images and a tender love story. The intention isn't to change awareness through the film's content, but instead just by having the film run.

Everywhere there's a forceful sense of how traumatized the young are. Judges are beaten up, school furniture is destroyed, and everyone in contact with young people has stories of apparently unmotivated outbreaks of violence. Perhaps the war's end has released a giant blister of built-up violence, which is now bursting in catharsis.

After we've sat around for a while, all of us men retreat to the guesthouse. One of the relatives comes over and crumbles some sticky black Afghan in the hollow of his hand. It then falls into a cigarette's emptied paper tube, which is twisted together at the end. It's given to me to smoke before bed. The unexpected happens.

The smoke is strong and spicy. It doesn't burn my mouth, nor my lungs, it raises my inner state, concentrates it, but then suddenly something occurs that hasn't since my getting stoned as a school kid. Fear materializes. A fear that rolls across the road, over the courtyard, out of the walls and floods me. Suddenly every fear that has ever been in this city is heading right for me. There's no enjoyable side to it, nor any way to evade it. It means business, it's a threat, intimidation.

If places solidify from experience, if they consist of everything that has ever been felt in them, then this fear is a kind of revelation. Kunduz is introducing itself. Inside this municipal area bombs have been dropped, rockets fired; rape, torture and murder have been committed. Snipers have lurked, scouts have searched houses for people in hiding, marauders have attacked and plundered, women have screamed, children have fled. Every possibility could be repeated. It's all too fresh. The violence isn't part of an archaic past, or a historical theme park. It's just not come visiting for a few days, and yet we're already talking about the peace.

The courtyard is dark. Only dogs and a few cars can be heard in the night. It's a different night, saturated in threat, a night in which so many lie awake in fear, as traumas return. There's the soldier's fear as he sees the wound, the victim's moment of utter helplessness, the destruction of a consciousness in deep shock.

Fear sits close to the marrow. It feels the geographical distance and the time I'd need to reach the arms of those dearest to me. I think of them, think of landscapes. Fear breaks through, fear without an object.

Hours later it all dissipates in amazement at what our heads can do – not at what they can think, so much as with what intensity they can make a feeling so physical and wholly unavoidable that it's suddenly an independent power.

Now the figures disintegrate, multiply, become inorganic and melt into mere structures and geometric patterns. My thoughts are suddenly hard to control, they stubbornly choose their own states. Then a wide brush paints a new mood, a Rothko red glows, a black wall rises up.

Or secondary lines flit away, each one asking to be followed, one after another, by which time the first has already been forgotten. Then all these visions dissolve in other pictures, landscapes, erotic scenes, a single unit of me wandering through organic and inorganic structures, no sooner does it touch the skin than it's gone through it. From erotic sights to medical ones. Then just spheres, space, *2001: A Space Odyssey*, lastly structures, patterns, scribblings, a damaged stencil.

I'm lying under a new blanket printed with big red poppies. It must be 100 per cent polyester, it crackles and sparks like a firework as soon as I move it in the dark, which I start to do with an increasing, simple sense of pleasure.

~

Early one morning. Nadia is sitting alone in the courtyard, in black and orange today. She's sitting in the arbour, has spread out a warm yellow blanket and holds a few rose petals in her hand and smells them from time to time. She's sitting in complete silence, the garden is just stirring. Then I realize that she's recording the sounds around her with a little microphone: the chirruping of birds, the banging of pans in the kitchen, people calling in a neighbouring house. Nadia's brother lives in the States. He hasn't been able to travel to Afghanistan for a long time. Now he'll get tapes with the sounds of his childhood haunts. We listen together to the new day beginning.

This magical garden hasn't lost any of its magic. On one side her aunt lives, on the other side another uncle. If they had a row, the connecting doors were bolted shut, but never for long. The girls enjoyed their games together, in which they tentatively explored the world of grown-up women. The local boys watched them secretly, or so they thought. For their part, they watched the local Sikhs who stood at their windows brushing their long hair.

Turab has placed a sawn-open bomb casing in his garden and is planting hanging flowers in it with a conspiratorial grin. A subversive gardener, in the past he has had wrangles with all the fundamentalists, including a Taliban judge. That evening he creates two forms out of dough.

'I'll call this one The Judge's Turban, because it's so convoluted. This other small one, that looks sort of crippled, what should I call it? I know: The Judge's Testicles.'

Mirwais, in his Afghan one-piece shirt and trousers, on top of which he's wearing both a Scandinavian patterned sweater with St. George sewn onto it and a jacket; Mirwais, with his fingers on his prayer beads and worry in his face, our protector with darting eyes and a tendency to search every room immediately for possible dangers; Mirwais, who doesn't let us go out alone or wander off, who always pops up as a negotiator and mediator and who checks every bridge to see if it's passable. He carries this special responsibility to keep us out of harm's way, although we almost don't realize it any more. He hasn't taken on this attitude, he is it completely. Protecting us is now his life, and he will only have his own life back when we leave the country unharmed.

He amazes us, someone who has survived the war, who demonstrates a father's care, an ideal mother's attentiveness: 'Was the water too cold?'

We talk to each other through interpreters, normally Nadia. Sometimes I just copy his Afghan sentences' sounds, and he gives a deep belly laugh. Today he only said two things to me: 'you aren't allowed to serve me' (I had passed him an ashtray), and 'you should learn Dari'.

But when I begin to ask him questions, he slowly starts to tell more. When he was 19 he fought the Russians with his friends, the mujaheddin. They won because they were mobile, never eating lunch at the same place where they'd had breakfast, and because their military strategy was based on surprise attacks and had the support of the general populace.

After the Russians were expelled, the various mujaheddin groups became involved in bitter infighting. This resulted in bloody feuds and violence of all kinds. Although Mirwais tried his hand as an interpreter and then a journalist, there was soon no one ready to support his work. So he withdrew. And now? He lives in the knowledge that his intelligence isn't needed or his morals. 'Today I'm a farmer, making sure that the birds don't eat the seed on the fields.'

He doesn't mention his work in schools and with the aid projects.

'But maybe you are just what's needed in politics.'

'There's certainly a need here. Politics is all crooked. Karzai doesn't have blood on his hands. That's the only good thing you can say about him. He didn't want to insult anyone, so he's got some of the worst sorts in government.'

'Parliament doesn't give you some hope?'

'Less today than a year ago. Once again the country hasn't got to be where it's at through its own efforts.'

A year ago the elections were still coming up. Right now the final results are expected any day now. The dribs and drabs of news people hear has crushed any idealism.

Once we've agreed on the ad's wording and written it down, it's taken by a messenger to the broadcasting building. Mirwais monitors its progress by mobile phone.

'You'll be inundated,' he says. 'The people here don't know what to do with their time.'

Turab is still sceptical. 'Maybe we should let men in too ...?'

Protests. Out of the question.

Our breakfast is on the lavish side: home-baked bread with a pattern stamped on it, eggs, quince jelly and Laughing Cow processed cheese that has somehow made it to Kunduz from distant Austria. We ask Khaled how German sounds to him.

'Not good, not bad, a bit like a sound you can't quite understand.'

And then there's silence again as they all start another journey into the province where they are most at home: that of memory. Yes, they still all live together in their past.

The messenger returns from the television building. The ad will be shown twice, at 5.30 and 7.30 this evening. The free film will also be announced over the PA system at each showing today.

Mirwais says, 'We need a film with shooting. People aren't interested in anything else.'

Nadia: 'We need films that change people's attitudes.'

We discuss the issue of whether the representation of violence changes people and we're immediately at the core of every debate on violence. Does the represented violence have a purifying and cleansing function, or does it serve as an initial model and incentive to violence? The theme is just as well debated here as on any German panel discussion where 'quality or quotas' are brought up, but the resonance given to it by 25 years of war means that it sounds different here in Kunduz than in Mainz.

What arrives from Pakistan at the local markets? Children's trumpets, machine guns with rapid fire sounds, inflatable pink deer, lighters in the form of hand grenades, violet and metallic blue tanks and motorized turtles wearing sunglasses. The first offerings from a world of excess to one of scarcity.

The wall of the old fortress towers above the stalls. Its

defensive ditches are dry, its sparse turf is scattered with the green remains of Soviet tanks. It was also the Taliban's military base in Kunduz. Battles raged over this last bastion. Today it's a walled plateau, empty and forgotten, just grass and rubble. It used to be where dog and cock fights took place. Today there's nothing here to remind people that commanders lived and soldiers died on this look-out hill, and that from here messages were sent all over the world. There's no way of knowing that the hill brought fear to people, evoked bloody visions, and was coveted by soldiers and camera teams hoping to seize it.

~

Outside Kunduz we pass the first mud buildings where former refugees live. They returned home from Peshawar along the road to Jalalabad, home to peace. But what do they find? Fields reclaimed by the steppe, their houses collapsing or destroyed by gunfire, and electricity and water supplies cut off. They join forces, assemble makeshift dwellings near a water supply and get down to the business of surviving.

The steppe spreads out, settlements scattered in it like oases. Nomads go past selling camel skins, goat's cheese and cloth. Children stream out, carrying water on their heads. They walk into the infinite distance, as if they were heading into the curve of the earth itself. Sometimes we see a pond, a bush surrounded by a few huts, or a walled courtyard, with a well and an oven squeezed in. There are old people who have learnt to fight firstly for their lives and now for their livelihoods, young people who are almost collapsing under the burden of everything they can imagine, of all the images of life that have been brought to them. All this grows in the desert, on rocks, in the dust, in almost nothing.

We turn onto the big black road that leads through the bright yellow steppe. An old man with a booming voice is in our car now. He knows secret routes to the shy Uzbeks, and knows the people themselves too. He'll try to help us to enter one of their villages. We drive on. There could be haze or hills on the horizon, or nothing. After 20 minutes we reach the first curve.

We turn off the paved road, onto – nothing. We drive over rolling ground, down dips, up hills, in a blizzard of dust and sand, then over the steppe, soft enough to yield like pressed straw underfoot.

Finally a little bulge ahead, a little rise in the horizon that turns into herds of sheep. They're tended by two shepherds, a young one asleep on a hump of sand and another trotting his horse leisurely in a circle, and three nasty dogs that have to stand up to wolves and jackals too. They're always ready to fight. During the war the wolves even ate bodies left behind.

The shepherds know that. The younger one slips off his hummock and comes a few steps closer. He's wearing a pullover, a padded green jacket and a pinstripe waistcoat under his felt coat. He uses his crook both as a support and to protect and herd the sheep. There are around 700 of them around here, watched by 10 to 14 shepherds, and at risk from tarantulas, snakes and jackals.

Where does he sleep?

'Somewhere in the steppe.'

What does he eat? He's strapped his bread to his back. Where does he draw water?

'It's a six-hour trek with the animals to the nearest spring.'

'And is your herd safe?'

'Sometimes thieves come and steal a few animals. But what should I do? We just steal a few back then.'

'And what would you do if I stole from you?' Turab would like to know.

'I know karate,' the shepherd says. His face says he's never joked in his life, or would like to give that impression anyway.

'What do you eat?'

'My bread smeared with fat that I carry around in this tub.' He shows it to us.

'And why do you stick around here,' Turab needles him, 'rather than look for proper work in the city?'

'I can't do that.'

He hears where we come from: 'You live in a good country. It always rains there.'

'What do you earn?'

'I earn a tenth of each year's lambs. If I'm lucky, that's 50.'

'How old are you?'

'I don't know. Maybe 21?'

'But you don't have a beard yet!'

'Can you tell me how old I am?'

Afghan conversations often go like this. In no time they're talking about how they live, indeed about intimate things. Never is a question refused or challenged. People share stories and the air they breath.

~

We walk on through the steppe. For a long time we see little more than the sweeping lines of settled dunes and dusty hollows, then from every direction children approach, as if out of thin air. They are carrying plastic pistols and Kalashnikovs – the first things that the children buy with their money; they don't know what disarmament is.

Then suddenly the atmosphere changes. The air becomes clearer, cotton fields and different vegetation appear, maize too. Behind straw palisades we can see a wall encircling the defensive squares in which each Uzbek clan arranges its huts. Trampled paths weave between houses and camels are led along dusty streets. The impression is of African mud houses, no different to those in Mali or Burkina Faso.

We stand in front of the gate and wait to see if we'll be let in. A ceremony is taking place somewhere. A bride is being fetched by camel, as is the custom, and brought to the bridegroom's house. A motorbike roars and yet we're on the edge of an isolated culture that has cut itself off from the world around it, a culture that threatens to suffocate in its poverty. While we wait a boy drives a matted camel by, accompanied by a mangy dog, followed by an old man on a woman's bicycle.

~

An elder bids us to enter his clan's square. He doesn't take his grotesquely fashionable sunglasses off, they're a status symbol to him. Our little retinue is followed by a boy carrying a jug of hot water and a bowl, for us to wash our hands.

The inner yard squeezes all the clan's activities together into one narrow space: there's a well, an oven, stables and a workshop. The last of these is empty when we come, because the women, who weave the famous Uzbek carpets here during the day, have retired now.

The clan's chief was kept prisoner in Kunduz for a long time. He mentions stoically that he was tortured, as if he'd have left out this fact, so standard in people's biographies around here, were it not for the sake of completeness. As he speaks he holds his turbaned head bowed and passes his delicate hand over the unfinished material in front of him, colourful fabrics that the children will then fold in practised movements. Even the soles of these children's feet still have henna decorations from the recent holy day. The elder offers us tea. 'Wait, I'll drink first, then you needn't fear anything.'

Once the caravanserai tea, that actually comes from China, was highly praised. 'It has folds like Tartars' boots, and rucks like the belly of a mighty ox, spirals like the mist that rises from a ravine, and it quakes like a lake that the blue sky caresses ...'

While we're drinking the children run out to call the council of elders together, and there they stand: 25 men, mostly in turbans, with long robes and dignified, even rather melancholy, faces, and among them Nadia. In a headscarf that shows her face she walks with them towards the communal building where she'll listen to the council's requests – now quite in her role as chair of her aid organization.

The hall has just been completed and is the pride of the community. In a bout of high spirits or idealism it's been decorated with bright blue clouds. It looks as foreign to its surroundings as a health spa would among nomads.

We're sitting in a circle on cushions. More and more men squeeze in from outside. Boys weave in and out with plates full of pistachios, almonds, dried fruit and pulses, and a few sweets in wrappers. All this happens without us having heard any orders. Nadia tells us later that behind the scenes people rushed out to look for a proper meal for us, but they didn't manage to find what they wanted.

Nadia scarcely has to start speaking and there's utter silence. The old men, fearing the future and clinging to what their traditions have given them, look out of their withered faces into Nadia's open face and see how much times change. They all knew her father though, and so they find it easier to listen to his daughter. They don't need to put their trust in her, they already trust her. But their requests are big – compared to what Nadia can offer: huge.

The light suddenly fades in the room. The old men bite open a few almonds, but keep their eyes on Nadia, trying to figure out whether she'll help them to have a deeper well dug, a school built, and a doctor hired for the local clinic, now empty.

Most diseases are waterborne. Sometimes animals die in the well and pollute the drinking water, sometimes uneducated farmers even throw a carcass into the shaft of the well. Malaria is rife too. Nadia listens to all of this as patiently as if it were the first time, and yet these stories are always much the same. They gaze without blinking at her attentive face. No one begs, no one complains, there's no wringing of hands, pulling out of hair, none of them lose their composure.

By selling carpets and animals they can scrape together a living for six months a year, in good years. During the second half of the year they get by on what they themselves have planted. As soon as the sun rises the farmers are in the fields or with their animals. They have bread and tea for breakfast, milk if they have any.

I write down what the farmer reports. Those in the room take note discreetly of what interests me. No sooner have I lowered pen to paper than all their eyes are trained on its nib. What is told here is just their normal life. What is there worth writing down? That mines on the fields pose a great danger? True, but nor is it easy to deal with wolves.

The happiest farmers are those who own an ox plough and have a cow that they can depend on. Such farmers can even afford fertilizer sometimes.

'But it tastes better without fertilizer,' I say, and everyone laughs, happy that strangers can agree so completely.

The conversation turns to agriculture, harvests, the late sown rice. We found a few poppies behind the school. Where might their seeds have flown from? The poppy fields are never visible from the roads.

'We don't plant poppies,' says the chief.

'We were told you've harvested 40 kilos from your fields,' calls out our middleman. Everyone laughs again, the chief even slaps our middleman on the shoulder in a friendly way.

But no, nothing here reveals secret affluence. The children often go to school at six in the morning, so that by the early afternoon they can be ready to help their parents with picking cotton or tending animals.

By now Nadia has started to draw up the proposal for a well on a page torn out of her notebook. As she does so, an elder recapitulates a typical farmer's day. After lunch, normally of rice, nothing else is eaten until evening prayers. Then there's bread and buttermilk.

'That stretches the belly and makes you tired,' says Nadia. 'You could say it's Afghans' alcohol.'

After the meal the men sit down with the women, knot carpets and tell each other stories. Sometimes the men also look after the babies, so that the women can work unhampered on the carpets. Because the men are allowed to marry several women, they also leave several widows behind, causing some villages to be kept going largely by women. In this village there's no television set, and only one person, the most well off of the farmers, has a generator. So people go to bed early.

'Has the weather changed over the years?'

'Yes. Over all, it's got warmer. So we have more pests, and the cotton harvests haven't been as good. Years ago we had much more snow.'

Worry doesn't leave their faces, which seem to have been passed down to them like their shoes. Their hands are cracked working tools, their feet too look leathery and worn thin. The tea tastes of the smoke in which it was made.

By now the proposal's been drawn up. Someone brings an ink pad and all apart from two of the men put their fingerprints on the block capital names that the secretary has written out. One man has a seal. Another turns to Nadia suddenly, and hisses, 'Help me, give me a moped!'

In the end Nadia is holding a dirty sheet of paper in her hand, dark with soot and fingerprints. In the near future a well is going to come of it. The head of the village elders holds out on his forearm three valuable coats of green and violet, the kind of coat Karzai wears. It would be impossible to refuse the gift. The old man himself says, 'We don't have anything, but what we possess and won't give away is our humanity and our pride.'

The river Oxus, stuff of myths. For centuries travellers have toiled to reach this river on Afghanistan's northern borders, often not managing, due to ambushes, lack of food, malaria, infestations of worms or epidemics. Robert Byron did finish the journey. He stood on the banks of the Oxus and went into raptures about it, remembering too the poor souls who died trying to reach it. Right now we are driving in a straight line north through the steppe, between rice fields and fallow areas to reach this end of the world.

A border guard is waiting at a rundown checkpoint. There's a little shop too, and a dishevelled man with a long beard, maybe an old hippie, certainly disturbed, is leaning on a railing. Scrap from the war lies between the huts round about. Rusting equipment in the fields. Nothing scenic, just a few stranded, forgotten people around a barrier.

The street ends at a gate. We're allowed to go through to enter the port area, or rather: the scrapyard that spreads out where an active river port must have been. Everything left behind by the war, all the rusting metal collected in the area, now sits in piles between warehouses, loading ramps and a monstrous crane that rises above the brackish water with the same operatic gesture that earlier ages found in the Industrial Revolution's mighty machines. It's like a Visconti stage, translated into the world of machine poetry, like a dignified monument to a 100-year-old technology that's slowly rusting away. The crane's arm is gesticulating blindly across the river, towards somewhere in Tajikistan.

And even the low Oxus seems to have adapted to its surroundings. Its banks are covered in silt and its water flows ponderously, although it has a strong undercurrent, revealed sometimes by streaks on the surface. Not long ago a rider and his horse wanted to reach the safety of the Tajik side of the river. They struggled heroically, the locals say, but both drowned.

Where the water has retreated wide mud banks are exposed, with gullies and shifting ditches between them. Upstream a little makeshift ferry bobs on the water. It has just moored in Tajikistan between a couple of drab industrial buildings and containers that carry on the spirit of the Afghan side. A posthumous landscape. A landscape after the withdrawal of all activity, remaining just as the guardian of an absent history. Yet as soon as you look east the steppe is there again, yellowy green and spreading unembellished into the distance.

The slightest thing could animate this muddle of dirt, ruins and war scrap. As if he knew this, an old man on crutches suddenly clambers over the port wall. His potato face bleats at the dusty grey sky. Birds fly up immediately, children shout in the distance. Then nothing more. Just the rattling of a piece of metal, a few voices carried on the wind, and from the birds that have nested in the crane a few listless noises that barely sound as if they're from birds. Footsteps in the gravel getting fainter. Khaled has spread out his prayer mat on the mud and is doing his devotions fervently. The silence of a day of rest suddenly fills the air, unreal, as if the end were nigh.

Carefully our little group walks to the water's edge. The place looks as abandoned as if nobody has come here in years. There's nothing beautiful here; a feeling of compression.

Among the desolate places I've been attracted to, this one has a particular effect on me. Go away, it says, there's nothing here, turn around, don't look, don't take anything with you, don't be here, evaporate – or something like that. I dip my hands into the yellowy grey, milky and shimmering water. It's like putting them in cold, liquid opal.

The quay wall is covered with a luxuriant layer of yellow lichen. A pontoon is floating there too, but it's probably not been used by a boat for years. Just one plastic blue chair has been left, facing the steppe: an echo of the border, the echo as the border. You turn around and you're immediately tempted to say: I just imagined that place.

~

And who doesn't look downriver where the scarce gold deposits still attract prospectors and where the opium is processed that just by crossing the river is worth many times what it was before? One of the Afghans who has joined us tells me of a German diplomat who smuggled 17 kilos of opium undetected in his luggage. He had sprayed it with a certain perfume that the sniffer dogs can't stand.

'How do you know that?'

'Because I sold it to him.'

A V-shaped formation of migrating birds is just changing direction above the river. A bridge is supposed to be built here, although the Afghan and Russian soldiers are vehemently against it. Even the authorities know that the bridge suits the drug smugglers best of all. A kilo of raw opium costs $3,000 on this side of the river, and $10,000 on the other side, which is only 500 yards away. Nor should anyone be under the impression that Tajiks and Afghans are carrying out this trade among themselves. One of the most influential players here is an American citizen. No one admits to knowing more. In the end two locals give away just his nickname: White Ibrahim.

~

As evening falls the shepherds drive their animals into the pens and the cowherds drive theirs along the ditches that go through the rice fields and run parallel to the road. Three boys have set up a little bike repair workshop there. They're wearing cardigans of the same colour as their turbans. Friends run up, a little of their henna-dyed hair showing under embroidered caps. An old man catches a lamb that had escaped and just tosses it back over the wall of his property before wading on to us.

Apart from that it's quiet at the road. Our car stopping draws all movement to it, a vanishing point. Now they're coming in our direction from distant houses, and even the cowherds halt with their cattle for a minute, while the sun throws the most beautiful late light over the water's surfaces.

The teenagers tell us that they have no jobs, and 'no future', as they quickly add. Two of them have just returned from the refugee camp in Peshawar to this region, their parents' home. They say they're 'dying of boredom here'.

Indeed, scarcely anyone finds assimilation as hard as these boys, who had never lived in their parents' poor home region and who have left behind the very different world of the refugee camps. Now they're supposed to start a new life on a road in northern Afghanistan with 2,500 other families, without electricity or a school. They smile their brightest smiles, beautiful but laced through with traces of fatalism.

'It's so boring here,' the youngest one says. 'I've had enough of life.'

The little children who come up to us in clothes like pyjamas have old widows' faces, watchful yet too mature, like buds that have started to wilt. Who talks about these children's undeveloped potential? If you ask them about what we call 'free time', they're amazed. You have to explain the word, and they can barely differentiate 'play' from 'eat' or 'tend the animals'.

One of the children leans up against his mother like a

fawn. Young animals express their love like this, as something essential. Everything about this child reminds you of a young animal, its tenderness shows no sign of experience, it's as needy as on the first day of its life.

~

Sunset on the steppe: the camel drover stands silhouetted with his eleven animals against the increasingly opalescent sky. His youngest camel is two years old, his oldest is six. We walk towards him in the dirty dishwater light that dusk begins in.

'Ay ha!'

The animals slow down, turn to look at him, and trot on, more slowly.

He leans on his staff, looking at us with the same gaze with which he watches his camels. Yes, they each have a different character, even moods. When they start trotting he sometimes has to run after them. Especially in winter they can get rather difficult, kicking out and biting each other, and you have to make sure they don't get injured. That's when they miss having room to run around. No, they don't have any natural enemies, just the mines. Jackals only dare to attack small sheep, and snakes can't harm them either.

'No one can beat a camel!'

By now the animals have drifted away. 'Aren't you at all worried that you could lose your animals while we're talking?'

His gaze turns patiently towards the steppe, grey-blue in the dusk. Then he just shakes his head.

It's another ten minutes before he grabs his coat and excuses himself, saying he has to tend his animals now. He walks off in the opposite direction to where his camels are. Only now do we find out that he also tends a herd of sheep, which by now is grazing far out of sight. He was too polite to pass without talking. As he goes he turns around once more, 'You're driving to Kunduz, aren't you?'

'Yes.'

He walks on, nodding.

The sun has left just one orange-grey farm on the horizon. The camels are trotting along towards where it's already night and black, the drover stays in the lighter patch. Now night falls silently, muffling the noise of dogs and camels. The camels' hooves don't make a sound or leave a mark on the springy ground. The barely visible new moon comes out, and Nadia says, 'On the first day of a new moon, people in the steppe kiss their fingertips and make a wish.'

We do too.

Is it now the most silent silence? It's as if someone had removed a glass dome from the steppe and wrapped it in a more spacious and festive sphere. A special atmosphere mixes in with the silence, filling it. Something enters it like breathless anticipation. A single, very distant dog's bark penetrates the quiet from somewhere, just to make the silence even more palpable.

~

The silence of the steppe: when you hear a noise in the distance you're where that noise is, in the distance. Seen like this, in the city all of us are placeless, surfing on short-wave reception and continually thrown to all possible distances. But when the steppe is completely silent, you're only where your own breath is, where your own steps are. So you're all there. Where you rarely are.

Arriving back in Kunduz we're already expected. An old woman has arrived to talk to the women of the house. She used to be their maid. Grief has been engraving itself deep in her face since the day years ago when her son went outside to buy something quickly. A bomb exploded right there in front of the house just at that moment. The boy died, the mother lost her life too. She's locked in a state of mourning, and clings to Nadia's shoulder, crying. The group of wailing women moves to the back room, the men are left on their own. Khaled tells us about Eid's rituals.

'And what do you talk about as you feast?'

'We tell each other who has died, who has married. That's the most important thing. That lasts a long time.'

'And then?'

'And then we say how Karzai has betrayed us all.'

'And who defends him?'

'No one. You can't praise a bald man for his beautiful locks of hair.'

'What do you blame him for?'

'That he's not brought any experts into his government, just the old gangsters, so as not to hurt anyone's pride. He only let the honest ones go.'

Every day this political analysis is repeated, no one tires of it, rather it strengthens the sense that they are in this together. Then one of them tells of Afghans who have tried to live as nomads but failed, and have now returned to the city's ruins; another tells of a teacher who had to be dismissed because he vented his trauma on his pupils. In what way? In despotic behaviour, beating and ordering them about excessively.

Turab's wife is expecting her child any day. She'll give birth at home.

'We're there,' says Nadia. 'Don't be worried.'

'But what can we do?'

'We'll shout: Push! Push!'

Sudden excitement in the next room. We have to come. The break with our cinema ad has just started. All the women in the house flee the television room, all the men make themselves comfortable on the warm cushions. Nadia translates. First a singing woman appears, who only moves from her hips, like a plastic doll. Until recently women weren't allowed to be shown singing or dancing on local television. This woman seems to be bickering more than singing. It's apparent that she's following instructions from off-screen.

Next a synthetically produced Afghan family appears, convincingly connected by blood and their Roshan mobile phones. Even grandpa laughs into his phone, as if he's just been told there's a ceasefire.

This is followed by a screeching singer in front of a heater lit by colourful spotlights. Indeed, all the colours around him merge in psychedelic effects.

Mirwais gets up. 'I'll just go to the station and ask about our ad.'

By now the music-and-ads programme has risked a daring cut to a houseplant and is zooming in on its leaves, where – thanks to the magic of the dissolve – the next singer is now appearing. He looks like a roving TV reporter in a crime series – and sounds like one too.

Then a pan to the otherwise unoccupied houseplant. In the

long run, however, there's not too much to look at here, so the disgruntled camera chooses to focus on the head and torso of the untiring singer. Yet by now his right eye has, for no obvious reason, drifted towards the root of his nose, while his half-length portrait shines in front of a wooden venetian blind no more visually attractive than the houseplant.

While we watch this sentimental show, at the door the old woman who lost her son says goodbye to Nadia, crying and laying her head on Nadia's shoulder, then kissing her hands, and then pressing a kiss on her heart through her dress.

Mirwais calls from the television station. They've already shown our ad twice, but they'll show it again now. Because Mirwais pressures them, they show it just before eight so that we can all see it.

A little later a static picture appears on television of a magnificently elegant water lily. A voiceover mourns a citizen's death, names those left behind and the day and time of the funeral. The photo remains, but the voice lightens a little as it proceeds, 'Free. A German humanist and friend of Afghanistan ...' The rest is lost in our cheering.

~

The nightly gatherings for debate. One of the men is a small, black-bearded man with restless beady eyes. He could be a Talib. He's the only one without a prison story. Is he a mole? He's quiet and there's something of the informant about him.

But on the other hand, if that were the case, how does he adapt? He's become a know-it-all, but he has a fundamentalist's reactions. He's continually offended by opinions the people around him are raising on politics, the cinema and women. From time to time he gazes furtively at Nadia, this tall unveiled Afghan woman, as if he were suffering from himself, from the light coming from inside himself. What's he hoping for?

~

We're talking about the captions for the Laurel and Hardy film. Nadia wants to go through them with me later tonight, so that she can read them out with a microphone from the back of the cinema. Impossible! Even Turab warns us against it. 'The cinema has become a place for junkies and ex-soldiers,' he says. 'You can't stand up there and talk. It's too dangerous.' Nor is there a microphone.

We decide that the children's film can be understood without captions too, and decide to go and choose the main film.

Turab phones around for the man with the key to the cinema. An hour later the man has arrived, but he doesn't have a key. Nobody gets flustered.

And how about the projector? It will be brought tomorrow morning from another province, in time for the showing at 2 p.m. And the main film?

'There needs to be fighting and shooting,' repeats Mirwais.

We insist as before on a real woman's film. The projectionist has two films to offer in this genre, both gentle films from India. The first is about a woman who lives alone with animals in the jungle ... We're not against the idea. A strong self-reliant woman, a female Tarzan, that could be good. Then I remember *Sheena, Shame of the Jungle*, or whatever it was called. 'Don't you think she'll appear naked within five minutes?'

Turab thinks that too would have educational value, but

when I imagine the 'German humanist and friend of Afghanistan' bringing nakedness meant for a Western audience into a disreputable northern Afghan cinema, then I'm no longer sure how humanistic it would be.

'And the other film?'

'It's a love story, I'd recommend it,' says the projectionist. 'It has an ambitious dramaturgy.'

Not the word 'ambitious', but 'dramaturgy' decides it. Someone who considers a film's dramaturgy must know something about cinema, so we should respect his recommendation. We decide on the romantic film and plan to have a look at the cinema the next morning.

~

I sit, surrounded by voices that I don't understand, in relationships that I can't clearly grasp, among people who have fought and killed, who have been taken captive and tortured, who life has thrown into incomprehensible positions and who history might grab at any moment and sweep to another spot. They talk as if with conviction, but their ideology isn't stable. They're guided only by their desires for peace, goodness, family harmony and the provision of their material needs – things common to all religious cultures.

~

Nadia is always still wide awake come evening, and yet the men withdraw at 10 p.m. As I'm not allowed to stay alone with her, Turab sometimes sits down with us on the steps in front of the guesthouse and smokes, while we talk. When he gets too cold, we go our separate ways.

Turab, with his zest for life, lighting one Pine Light after another, and finishing every story with a punchline, takes his two girls to school every morning, one in red and one in green. They walk along with their heads bowed, holding his hands. What idyll will they tell about one day? Will they break into tears at the sound of horses' bells?

I look at the old photos that Turab saved at some personal risk, for photos of people were forbidden under the Taliban. On the oldest photos Nadia's father with his melancholy eyes, his high forehead and keenly concentrating face looks like a nomadic nobleman from another century; on the later photos he looks like an Egyptian nabob in his Western suit.

Nadia's mother is a beautiful, high-spirited woman. On each picture her inner life illuminates the play of her facial gestures, as she smiles and shows the sensitivity that Hans Christian Andersen captured in his sentence: 'I am like the water. Everything moves me, everything is mirrored in me.'

On one photo she's standing dressed as a man next to two warriors: a tall, thin boy with a certain androgynous charm. On another the parents are out on a hunt, both wearing traditional costumes of Afghan men.

It was decreed in 1959 that women needn't wear the veil. In the following years women were legally recognized as equals in the constitution, and women sat in parliament. The present can't carry on from there, it must work to regain that liberality. The next photo I look at shows Nadia's volleyball team playing against a team chosen by the maths teacher. In those days the pupils often played against the teachers.

On other pictures the family can be seen in the steppe with a big tent, then the sisters decked out in bombastically colourful folkloric dresses, smiling constrainedly under their towering hats and ornaments, as if they were trying to balance it all.

Next come pictures of fancy-dress balls, including women in short skirts and with fake beards painted or stuck onto their faces. Others have billowing dresses from the Fifties and diadems – a shift in fashions parallel to that which occurred in our part of the world. On other photos I see the sisters in a swimming pool, at the theatre, and dancing, playing or horse riding in lavish gardens.

The stage is still here. But life slipped away long ago and is just now tentatively returning.

~

The early morning is fresh and humid, evenings become cool as soon as the sun has gone down. It's Sunday today, but you wouldn't know. The birds are charging about in the trees. Below them some people are waking up to pressures, some to deadly boredom and some to a fight for survival. Who in this country leads what we call an 'ordered life'? Who here dies what we call a 'natural death'?

~

Nadia talks more and more about returning to Kunduz to dig wells, build schools, supervise projects, and to picnic in the flowering steppe in April. She is beaming non-stop: I've never seen her smile like this in Germany.

~

Our film plans suddenly seem to be on a knife-edge again. We've been warned of a possible attack, such as was carried out against another entertainment event recently. Perhaps someone aims to thwart 'their women' from being brought into the cinema, perhaps someone will use 'certain forces' against the show. Women too have expressed the fear that a bomb could explode in the cinema. It wouldn't be the first time.

Why don't you show the film in a school instead, someone suggests. No, if the cinema is to be reclaimed for women, we can't show the films elsewhere. We can't give in to pressure!

Nadia insists on inspecting the venue herself. She wants to check under every seat. But this time it's Mirwais, usually the most cautious, who brushes away our concerns. We walk over to the cinema. It's like the old suburban picture palaces – spacious, with wooden flip-up seats and a wide stage in front of the screen. It's painted light blue and has thin pillars which hold up the balconies on either side of the projectionist's room at the back. The little girls used to sit on the balconies and watch secretly. When they giggled all the men in the cinema would turn round but the girls ducked into the dark, quick as lightning.

From the screen to the front row is a mere fifteen yards. A small flight of steps leads up to the stage. A neon light and two naked bulbs scatter a diffuse light that barely reaches the room's corners. Yet we still check under the seats, walk around the room and talk to the projectionist in his cubbyhole. The film projector is still on the way, but it will be here on time. The DVD projector for the Laurel and Hardy film has been installed. We're ready.

~

Just half a day until the showing and we head north out of town. Further, further. If you follow this road you come to China. We cross the Three Waters River, pass rice terraces, okra fields and hollows with little streams where camels and sheep are brought to water. We turn onto dusty tracks along which little girls are walking to school. We too are on the way to a school, the one whose foundation stone was laid by Nadia and her co-workers two years ago, and which now accepts 800 children from 12 villages. All the children also have farm work to do, taking food to their fathers in the fields and feeding animals. Some have to walk a whole hour before they reach the sign at the school's entrance that says 'Knowledge and Skills Take People Further'.

The classes are characterized by an old-fashioned discipline that is strange to me. Everyone stands when a visitor enters the room, when greeted they answer as one, and they don't allow themselves a whisper or laugh. Their big eyes show complete concentration, and whoever is at the board bobs along with the pointer from letter to letter, reading the lines loudly and clearly.

A hygiene poster has been put up for the mixed class of young children, next to a board with the timetable and illustrations of mines. A little boy in a blouson and cap does his task seriously and confidently. The next one stumbles over a sentence: 'If you respect people, you will be respected by people.' His small face loses all colour, he has to return to his seat. No one so much as stirs.

'Which of you can read?'

Every hand shoots up. I ask the littlest child how old she is. She hasn't prepared that lesson, she doesn't know. The teacher comes over, holds her mouth and inspects her teeth. 'She's about eight years old.'

~

The girls' teacher is a very sad woman with grey hair who used to teach in Kabul. Then her husband was moved to the north of Afghanistan and she started teaching in this region, secretly when nothing else was possible, even in private and at 2 a.m. She risked her freedom and her health, perhaps even her life.

'When the Taliban were there, we weren't allowed to learn. When the Russians were there, we weren't allowed to learn to be Muslims. Today we're allowed both.'

Her husband died in the war, one of her sons too. Now she feeds her five children with the meagre wage put together by the Ministry of Education and the Afghanischer Frauenverein (Afghan Women's Organization).

All the children in her class can read. Sometimes younger girls accompany their older sisters to school and so learn too. The teacher and her pupils are the same, in that almost all the children here are orphans or have lost one parent. They've seen injuries, murders and dead bodies. Half the class has already had malaria. She herself, admits the teacher with a pained look, has mental health issues. Her own trauma, however, helps her to deal with the traumatic experiences the children have had.

The girls are calmer than the boys, who are more destructive and less under control. As soon as they reach puberty, the boys and girls have to be taught at different times, one group in the morning, the other in the afternoon. Added to this, come ethnic problems between Dari and Pashto speakers, between Turkmen and Tajiks, and everything else that can divide tribes and sectors in society. At least a school uniform has been introduced now – one that erases differences but doesn't get dirty easily. That's important, many people here don't have soap and so one reason they wear dappled clothes is because stains aren't visible.

And what do they want to become? The first girl: a doctor,

the second: a teacher, the third: an engineer. Another wants to work for the government, two others want to be painters.

'And what about an actor? or singer?' I ask.

The younger ones find that strange. It's not easy to contradict a stranger, but no, absolutely no one here wants to be either of those.

But what can they be? If their parents want, the girls can go to university and get an academic qualification – if the parents can afford that. The girls are needed for work in the fields, for embroidering items that earn them a little extra, and they have to be married off lucratively in order for the parents to have something to get by on.

And what does the girl at the board want to do when she's finished learning?

'Carry on learning!'

Sometimes this girl has even taught, when no teacher happened to be present. She stood in front of the mixed-aged class, which is for all those who haven't learnt to write and have their first chance now in peace-time. An educationalist might find this attitude to teaching exemplary, but it's like this only because what they learn is food to them.

Kunduz's one-horse carriages are magnificently decorated, the horses have studded bridles, red plumes and ringing horse bells straight from *Doctor Zhivago*. Among other uses, they carry passengers. Like trams in Germany, they've made it to our time from a pre-war era. I wonder whether the driver (who now and again gets up in the night to make sure that his horse, all he has, is all right), whether he himself drove through the war with this horse and carriage?

'Of course, I drove all through the war. How else could I have earned a crust for myself and my horse?'

That's another story: the owner of a plumed horse and carriage trotting through the war to the sound of horse bells.

When we arrive at the cinema at 1 p.m. a crowd has already formed, a rowdy crowd of jostling men. The two guards at the entrance and the few employees inside have their hands full.

'A woman! A woman!' a little boy shouts, as Nadia and I make our way through the men.

To discuss the situation we move to the delightful projection room. Its eight square metres are decorated with Koran suras, plastic flowers, textiles, Massud galloping along in the Panjshir Valley, Massud riding triumphantly into Kabul, and a photo of the Kaaba. Rolls of film lie below the two big old projectors. Nadia is negotiating bravely.

The right projector has been set up, the film is there. Laurel and Hardy can be shown too, and our woman's film is advertised outside with a poster. What worries us is the growing crush outside. We decide to let children in already.

So the man with the booming voice steps outside and announces that children up to 10 can go in. Some hesitate, some don't know exactly how old they are, others want to accompany their younger brothers or sisters inside. There's no end to the wrangling, it gets louder.

Nevertheless the security guards manage to separate the young ones from the teenagers. A small line of younger children trickles through the cordon and into the dark interior of the room. Up on the first floor I run to the window overlooking the entrance, so that I can see the surging crowd from above, then to the women's balcony to see the children come piling in. They immediately occupy the front rows. There's still no sight of a woman, either in the cinema or in front of it.

They whistle and shout. A sudden burst of music sounds shrilly, then falls silent. A scrap of film on the screen receives a cheer, but then fades away, before jumping back and starting again.

Outside the seething mass of adolescents is getting dangerously large. The ones at the back are pushing forwards, forming groups and lines and look like they're about to storm the cinema. If they did, who knows what would happen, but we can picture what we'd have on our hands if there were an incident here just because we'd set our mind to bringing women into the cinema.

'We're children too!' the teenagers shout in a very unchildlike way. We decide to ease the pressure by opening the lower seating to all men, but keeping the balconies reserved for women.

In a flash every seat in the room is taken. It's been a long time since that's been seen here. Now some even sit by the walls and on the aisle floor. The eager stream of people has flooded the room. When I look down onto the street outside again, there are only a few undecided people. No woman near or far. It's five to two.

'They'll come at the last minute,' says Nadia. 'When the others are already inside. They'll come then.'

A sporadic whistling rises from the room below. It's getting louder. Now and then there are tussles, but nothing serious, nothing frightening. Behind the curtain the sound system is screeching, then a few shadows flit across the screen and everyone goes silent, but it's just as silent on the women's balcony where I'm sitting on my own.

Things being as they are, I'm jittery about the prospect of presenting this expectant and not exactly peaceful crowd with a silent film by Laurel and Hardy. We discuss it in the projection room and decide, in view of how few of those in the cinema would probably appreciate the children's film, that we'll not show it for now.

An ear-splitting triumphal cry as a dancing couple appear onscreen, moving in time to the music, then sliding onto the stage floor before springing up towards the ceiling and disappearing. The Indian music, without any bass tones, almost tears the sound system apart, but turn it down, and it's almost lost in the hum coming off the speakers.

Silence. A black screen. Whistles and cheers of approval from the viewers. By now red laser beams from the telescopic sights of plastic toy guns are dancing over the screen. Now a man and woman return from the twilight to play chess. No sooner is there a full-length shot than the laser beams search out the woman's feet and scribble around in them. If she stands up, more lights go on and intrude electronically on her upper arms, her thighs, her lips, her breasts and between her legs.

Nadia and I watch these test runs from the balcony. We're still alone there. Nadia is recording the sounds for her brother in the States. It's an amazing din of quarrels, curses, cheers, laughter and threats. At a quarter past two there's complete silence. The actual film has started with some heavy-handed piano music and the announcement of the death of two soldiers.

It's getting very stuffy on the balcony from the rising breath of so many people. Whatever materializes on the screen from the projection beam's fog of colours is followed with open mouths. From time to time people's heads turn round, curious to see if women are on the balconies yet. Nadia, no one else.

Now a woman appears on the screen and it's suddenly so quiet you could hear a pin drop. She walks through a park as deafening music starts up. The points of light sweep towards her breasts and legs. The woman walks down streets and floats up and down flights of steps. She writes a cheeky 'I love you' without any apparent motivation on a classroom blackboard and walks on. The red laser beams escort her, and they know what they want more than she does. She's forgotten immediately as officers appear onscreen, then a helicopter drops off a man at night, and another rushes above a rubber dinghy towards a warship.

'Maybe the women are just missing the start and they'll come soon. That way they won't be seen,' says Nadia, ever hopeful. 'I've heard lots of them say they're coming.'

A local actor has joined us in the projection room. While the film carries on running inexorably, we sit on the floor and he tells us about the sketch shows he produces. They're about a simple and naïve man from the country, about quacks who charge extortionate fees, young men who can't find wives, and a man who wants to commit suicide but doesn't have the guts.

'People only laugh about things they know. We don't film love stories, but women are allowed to act in our educational films – if they dare.' Which is seldom the case.

On the other hand, we hear there's no real difference between Afghan and American cinema. 'The major difference is just that we only have one camera and no real stage sets, lighting and all that technology. Dialogue is better in American films too, whereas we improvise a lot. But apart from that ...'

When I return to the women's balcony Turab's wife, whose pregnancy is well advanced, and her two children are sitting there alone. What they're watching is war.

'Be careful, it's a cinema in there!' was the well-meaning warning she was given at the entrance, to which there's no answer – she knows what the cinema's like nowadays.

If the actors talk for too long, whistling rises to a crescendo. If a woman appears, it goes silent. And what an extravagant amount of young women in this film! Phones ring in the night and they start up in their nightdresses, rolling over towards the phone in a wanton manner.

The street in front of the cinema is quiet now. No woman or girl anywhere to be seen. Wolf whistles and feet stamping inside.

'But at least we've shown men the world of women's films,' I say, for now even Nadia has lost hope.

The screen shows heavy shell fire in a swarm of laser beams. We leave. Turab's wife follows us five minutes later. Only, we later hear, because she found the film boring.

'No woman!' a man in the foyer shouts at me, not in anger but in triumph, as if he's proud of the women of Kunduz.

As Nadia comes down the steps the projectionist gives a regretful shrug of his shoulders. 'The cinema's just not like it used to be.'

We didn't manage it, not at all. Once outside I see the poster for our woman's film. It shows the larger than life face of a hate-filled warrior, beside it and smaller a swaggering boy holding a submachine gun, then very small a beau with a silk neckerchief, and then a bombshell in a bikini. We didn't see the whole film, but who could doubt that its dramaturgy was for women?

Buzkashi, the wild horseback sport originally from Mongolia, was once part of wedding ceremonies here. As a 19th-century anthropologist reported, 'The young bride in her wedding dress mounts a fiery racehorse and spurs it into a gallop. She holds a freshly slaughtered lamb or kid goat on the pommel of her saddle. Her bridegroom and other men who are present try to catch up to her, but she has to evade her pursuers through skilful manoeuvring, so that none of them get close enough to tear away the animal she holds pressed to her chest.'

Until the game has been co-opted for tourists, it will remain a sporting and therapeutic event for the locals: dangerous and wild, an ancient tradition very much alive in the present.

We leave the centre of Kunduz. Clouds of dust hang over the half square mile of a sandy arena on the edge of the city. Slopes with a sparse covering of grass form natural terraces on two sides of the arena. Thousands of people are squatting close together here in beige and white, in baggy trousers and jackets, in turbans, caps and tied cloths, some of them wearing riding gear, others sliding their prayer beads between their fingers or shouting excitedly towards the arena where riders and animals tangle in a confused whorl.

The dust is materialized atmosphere, it wafts between the riders, floats over the slopes and colours faces, creating a sfumato effect over the plain. Sometimes horses' heads rise above the haze, sometimes a rider hanging from his mount's flank circles round near the crowd, sometimes another dashes into the heat of the action and is immediately flung out again, as if by a centrifugal force, where a single rider manages to keep the hide of an unrecognizably battered calf just far enough off the ground that it doesn't get caught up in the hooves. Whips are raised. The hennaed manes and tails sweep traces of rust and red into the clouds of dust, while right on the edge, where the energy ebbs, magnificently kitted out old men in warriors' costumes, audience members on horseback in fact, ride round the crowd looking for the best vantage point.

Then the pack of riders lurches forward and sweeps to one side, thinning out until it stops, bunches again and forms a melee over a new, equally unstable centre. A single loudspeaker on a pole booms out over the onlookers. Someone provides a rather unenthusiastic running commentary on what can barely be seen. The crowd only really erupts when the pack moves forward for a sustained period and someone manages to tear ahead for a few hard-won yards. In no time at all the carcass is yanked from his hands though, and the next rider storms off, collecting dust and tearing around in a mad zigzag holding his trophy at arm's length.

The dust billows and hides the horses' silhouettes, then the crimson-embroidered horse blankets are glimpsed, the light grey of prancing hooves, the horses' wide, panicking eyes. It's much more than a game. These are valuable horses, unbridled and half-wild stallions. Yet each is trained to filter from the chaos of orders backed up with crop and whip the one that orders it to position itself so that its rider can duck and grasp the corpse for himself.

By this time I'm standing in a huddle of people who're trying to see the spectacle through my eyes, and to look wherever I look. If I were to turn around and look at the audience, then 50 heads would also turn around too and inspect it. What is there to see there?

Nadia, who was the only woman in the whole arena, has had to be taken to the car already. People were grouping around intrusively. Yet since the pack of riders sometimes comes very close, scattering everyone in the area in all directions, she has a good view too. With her window wound down, she also asks the staring teenagers about what's going on. For them she's the only real spectacle here.

There's a lively to-and-fro on the stands. Bets are placed, meetings arranged, and embroidered horse blankets spread out for picnics. Young teenagers spit in the sand like adults. Once a heavy Mongolian's horse almost bolts. It rushes towards the stands, he forces it round just in time, but then it storms into the fleeing crowd in blind anger.

The sun is just a disc behind the dust, which starts to sink in blues and greys, its whirls catching the eye wherever riders spur on their horses.

Two boys have snatched the flayed carcass off a veteran rider. They hold it between themselves until one feints one way and then goes the other, pulling the animal his way and cheering as he completes a lap. The 18-year-old, a daredevil Turkmen, has won. He makes his horse rear up in front of the stands while the loudspeaker celebrates his victory, Afghani notes rain down on the crowd and his prize money to the value of £300 is announced.

The victor brings his mount round to the steep terraces again, a torrent of applause meets him, the wild rider, and he acknowledges it like an old hand. People start to drift off across the open arena and motorbikes are kick-started, while little girls still wander through the crowd with pots of tea, offering a cup of tea for two Afghani.

'Do you like horses?' I ask one of them.

'No, they frighten me.

Now and then during the war, instead of a calf's carcass the body of an enemy prisoner was used.

8

Over the evening pilau Turab reports that apparently around 50 women turned up at the cinema, but intimidated by the sight of the horde of men they quickly retreated. Could we have prevented so many men appearing?

The man with the booming voice cuts in. 'You saw it for yourselves today – young people have been damaged by the war. You could have had real trouble.'

'We couldn't have stopped them coming,' Turab says. 'The men are so starved of the sight of women that they were bound to come, even if only to stare.'

~

That evening we watch a snowy broadcast of the Indian Oscars. It may be from years ago. Television programmes have to be cheap here, so you never know which are current and which are well-kept antiques. You're a contemporary of many different years here. The Indian prizewinners beam modestly, they're thankful to be able to please their public. It's just the same as elsewhere, but here it has the ring of the distant future.

Afghan television is above all a museum of different people. It preserves its specimens in a murkily-lit solution of matt green tones. No one talks aggressively or directly at the camera. Rather, most people look as if they had hoped television would let them disappear.

~

Nadia's uncle had loved television with a passion, albeit an unrequited one. He set up more and more aerials, but was never rewarded with reception. One day after weeks of waiting a single picture appeared of a landscape in Tajikistan that he recognized immediately. Admittedly it disappeared the next instant, but the magic had delivered on its promise. A picture from afar had arrived in her uncle's living room and he sat in awe in front of the machine that had fetched that distant landscape for a few short seconds.

~

After the meal I try on a burka. How easy is it to move around in it, how much will I see? My first impression is that it's awkward and hot, my field of vision becomes blurred through the mesh and narrow as a pipe, the opening is that small. Not having had any practice, I need to be led along the street.

Sometimes women tug at the eye openings with their hands, on which they've put jewellery beforehand, if they haven't painted them with henna motifs. It's a way of showing who they are. One effect of the burka is certainly to encourage women to be creative.

Christian, our photographer, slips into a burka and ventures a few cancan kicks. It looks so strange that everyone laughs, as if present at an exorcism. Christian, the mad burka dancer. Mirwais warns him, 'If the husband wears his wife's burka, then she'll be the one wearing the trousers!'

It's our last evening in Kunduz. Our host's pride prevents too much sentimentality. Turab will stay here and cheer other visitors with his jokes, his wife will give birth soon and the old man with the booming voice will help to rebuild Kunduz. People will wait for the rice to ripen and will harvest the almonds, the winter will be hard and then in spring the steppe will burst into bloom and everyone will say that now's the best time for a picnic.

'You must come back then. We'll put up a tent and spread out blankets and sleep on the steppe at night like we used to do. That'll be wonderful.'

And so that we don't notice how choked he is, he laboriously lights another Pine Light and studies the slogan 'American Taste' on the box. This time there's no joke.

Everyone says that the peace is on thin ice. No one trusts the weapons' silence. Every day brings new reports of fighting in the south. Half the population still lives abroad, many of them are well-educated and would like to return, but they want conditions to improve, for example, for property disputes to be settled and for women's education to develop. And then, how will the un-traumatized exiles get along with those marked by decades of war?

Four children are playing with marbles in front of a burnt-out tank. When we approach they freeze. A girl says with fatalistic readiness, 'You've come to hit us.'

'Why would we do that?'

Mirwais explains that since the Taliban banned all games, children have come to expect to be punished for playing.

Poverty uses the same architectural forms everywhere, the same earthen cubes, the same slit windows, roofs of straw and mud, and high garden walls, rounded on the top. Glass is rare, tiles are only for the rich, and only the front gate is painted with a profusion of colours. All the painter's ingenuity is used in its patterns, so that among so much that looks the same, there's something that makes each place unique.

In the village children sift through the rubbish with a magnet, looking for tins. They also grab old bread, which they'll crumble into flour at home and bake again.

Now they encircle the car, staring at Nadia. They can't leave her alone.

'Don't you have a mother, little girls?' she asks them. They stay. There's nothing about her they don't find interesting. More and more join them to look at her, they can't get enough.

'Why are you embarrassing me in front of our guests?' That helps. But then others push towards us, teenagers and men too, and the mood turns into an ugly mixture of aggression and curiosity.

'What are you doing here?' they ask.

'We're interested in how you live.'

'Huh, leave us be, we'll get by all right.'

Just yards away an ISAF poster in a glass cabinet. It displays photos of heavily armed soldiers under the flags of their respective countries. They've been placed on a map, on the province where they're serving. Illiterates would only see aggressors in this image of the protecting power. Violence claims every region.

Not far from the road a nomadic family has pitched camp. Their three grey tents woven from goat's hair are low and wide. Inside them are high piles of carpets, canvases and woollen blankets. The women turn their faces away, an old woman mumbles to herself. The head of the family has four sons and six daughters, all with the same wife. His brother and sister also live with them. Just ten days ago a child was born here.

Another brother lives in the next tent with his family of nine sons and two daughters. To feed them all we only see a little soup cooking on the open fire and a portion of pulses and some bread beside it. They own about 30 animals – cattle, sheep and two donkeys. Now and then the nomads sell an animal, but only the males. They're self-sufficient. They do their own baking and slaughtering, and barter for what they can't make.

The leader's wife would like to become partially settled, with a summer camp near the Salang Pass, where it's cooler, and a winter camp in the south. But can the master of the tent leave his past behind that easily?

He slowly shakes his head and his thick white beard, chewing tobacco all the time as if he has a lot on his mind. He comes from a long line of nomad leaders. The nomads too, he proudly tells us, supported the troops against the Russians. They found food and fought. The war didn't affect them as badly as some. But in its wake rustlers, robbers and marauding bands arrived. They lived fearing something might happen to their children, and so hid the women, and tried to remain as inconspicuous as possible.

And they carried on working, as if it were more important than ever in these times to hold onto their nomadic traditions:

weaving, embroidery, working with felt and leather, tending the animals and producing some of the goat's cheese that the old man rushes to put into my hands. It comes in walnut-sized balls that are slightly warm and slightly grey from having been kneaded by hand. They taste of earth and goats, are a little spicy and so soluble that thrown in water they turn it into a cheesy soup. Water for washing, though, can only be spared once a month.

The old woman sits to the side, her lips quivering, her gaze elsewhere. A commotion sweeps through the tent. They're obviously used to living with the wounds of the past, others' wounds and their own. An unkempt little child climbs down from a pile of blankets; she's decked out in heavy, colourful clothes with braid trimming. Another peels himself out of a hammock.

They still live the nomadic life and are on their way to the southern provinces where the winter isn't as harsh, but where war's still raging.

'Give me medicine for my foot,' the disturbed woman mutters at us. We fetch a few anti-inflammatory remedies and painkillers from the car, as well as clothes that we can do without.

Rain clouds are drawing in from the mountains. The sky is getting greyer, only the children's colourful clothes still brighten up the dismal atmosphere. They've run out to collect fuel for the fire, mainly wood and straw stuck together with dung, and from a distance they look like mountain flowers.

They know all about tarantulas, snakes and scorpions, they can recognize the tracks of the wolves and jackals that steal close to their animals at night. They've lost a good many sheep to wild animals and mines, but even the 16-year-old who takes care of the turkeys acts with the same calm towards danger as the old man, who we learn is only 46 years old. His life has prematurely made a wrinkled old man of him.

Mirwais often worked with nomads when he was in the mujaheddin. They could work well together, he says, but they were too restless to let themselves be led. As they didn't take orders, they were given the task of transporting weapons, and allowed to chose their own routes.

'If you want to insult a nomad, you have to say: God keep you in a room with four walls! That's the worst. It really works.'

~

On the way back to Kabul we again pass by the house of the old General who Khaled has told us so much about. Didn't he provide his people with the picnic place where we were welcomed with a meal? Didn't he invite us so insistently to tea that it would be an affront not to go now? We climb up the slope. The house is well protected where it stands in a close knot of houses. The others aren't as big. In his own, two rooms have even been joined together to form a room as large as a meeting hall.

'We've already heard of your generosity. You've given the people here the picnic place where we were welcomed so warmly on our journey out.'

He plays it down. 'We have three yards of earth and four yards of sky. How can we be generous here?'

~

Once we're in Kabul, Nadia becomes more preoccupied. She's still dragging her roots behind her. We look for a restaurant where we can still eat at seven in the evening. In Haji Baba the food arrives lukewarm, but Mirwais defends the chef.

'The war changed our eating habits too. We used to eat into the early hours of the morning. Then a curfew was put in place from nightfall. So we ate at five, to be home in time. People haven't changed yet. We don't live under house arrest any more, but we still eat before it gets dark, just to be safe.'

Driving to the hotel in the dark we see an old man praying on the central reservation of the trunk road.

A terrible night in a different room of our old hotel. The bed's too short, and right in the blaze from two electric heaters. The worst thing is that the bed seems to be right in the flow of traffic. Every vehicle passes right through the room. I can tell petrol engines apart from diesel, single-cylinders from two-strokes, I hear lorries' and buses' four-tone horns, souped-up motorbikes, mopeds, even the difference between Toyota and Mercedes horns. I try the old trick of not fighting the noise but accepting it.

It doesn't help. I try lying with my feet to the window. After an hour I push my bed over to the door, dragging the mattress away from the window, into the corner of the room where light streams in from the corridor through the rippled glass of a fanlight. Nearing three in the morning it quietens down outside, then around half past four, before the muezzin's call, traffic starts to trickle back onto the streets.

I leave the room and venture outside. A young soldier meets me at the gate to the street. We exchange a few words of broken English. I ask him about his education. Hours later Nadia translates his answer for me: 'We're all burnt by the war. I can't do anything, anything at all.'

For some time I've been researching a book of interviews with former Guantanamo prisoners. I hear that it might be possible to talk to the man who had been the prisoners' spokesperson in the camp – and that just a month after his release.

'He was Afghanistan's ambassador to Pakistan under the Taliban. He hasn't given any interviews yet, and won't give any more. But if you're lucky ...'

My source, the last link in a long chain of middlemen, had been an important Taliban official. Nadia talks to him on the phone a number of times. None of us has seen him. Mirwais knows our plans and is concerned.

The middleman becomes ever more monosyllabic on the phone. We start to doubt that we'll ever see him. Then he suddenly agrees and wants to set up a meeting. He won't come to our hotel or give a contact address. But if we wait in a certain part of the city that evening, he'll call us and give us an exact meeting place.

When Nadia left Kabul University and arrived in Osnabrück, taking up Media Studies, she would start conversations with a good salvo of questions like any Afghan: 'How are you? And your family? Your parents, are they well? Your aunts? Yes? And your cousins? And how about your grandmother, how's she?'

The person she'd be talking to would explode, 'What business of yours is my grandmother?!'

Nomads are on the edge of Kabul too. No entry. Their tents

carry the mud architecture we've seen into textiles. They've come from the south, but they don't have any land here, not even space to set up camp. The roads have washed them here with their few animals, their trades and skills, their timid way of life. Between the tents old men are leaning on each other, there's a gypsy with a costumed monkey, an old woman selling honey she's collected herself, and animals and children with matted hair.

The chief of the 60 households stands at the entrance, a corduroy jacket over his smock. He doesn't budge: we aren't allowed in.

Soon he's giving my questions roundabout answers in a way we've come to expect in Afghanistan.

'What makes your life hard nowadays?'

'I'm an old man on the road.'

We let some time pass before returning to the question: 'And if we can call your life a hard one, what makes it hard?'

'The soil is poor, we don't have anything, we don't know where we'll stop tomorrow. Inshallah.'

We digress, looking out over the countryside as we talk, before asking for a third time, 'It might be thought your life is easier now, but what makes it so hard?'

'We aren't allowed to settle anywhere. The government leaves us in the lurch. I can't feed my children. The weather has changed. The winters are bitterly cold. The mines scare us. And our animals get stolen …'

And so it continues. Each issue isn't simply revealed to us once, rather it's developed, unfolded and carried from verse to verse. The day after tomorrow they'll move on, it'll get too cold in the city. Before then they have to sell a few sheep (making about one euro profit on each animal).

'But what a beautiful ring you're wearing!' I say, pointing to the tourmaline set in gold on his left hand.

'If only it were real!'

A child toddles over. Holding a patchwork doll in her arms, she looks like a patchwork doll herself. But no, it's not a doll, but a baby with downy henna hair and her eyes made-up.

'Are you worried about the children here in the city?'

'We've set up a guard and don't let the children go into town. What is there for them to do in the streets anyway? They should stay here.'

A sheep at his feet has started to sneeze. The girl hits its dusty hindquarters until it stops and traipses off grumpily. The little girl looks up with a triumphal expression on her wrinkled face.

Will she ever have a teacher? If so, the teacher would have to join the nomads and share their hard life.

'No, not even the NGOs help us.'

Smoke's rising and mixing with the smell of dung and something rotting. It blurs the view of the brand new Seiko billboard opposite the camp's entrance.

Nearby the refugees' tents are even more colourless and wretched. Sheep and goats are driven between the camps and into town. There they'll bolt between stalls where others of their kind hang in pieces. Some are still bleeding into the buckets below. Other refugees duck into ruins on either side. They've replaced the missing roofs with canvas.

~

'Where you're from the rich live in the mountains, here the poor,' says Mirwais, and laughs.

A Filipino woman once said to me, 'Rich people in your

country want to be brown, ours want to be white. Your rich people are silly.'

'True,' Mirwais agrees.

The huge campus of the girls' school lies on the edge of town, near the old Russian blocks of flats built for government officials and soldiers. Around 5,000 girls are given a primary, middle and secondary education here, about 50 a year manage to continue on to university.

The school director is a tough woman. She's positioned her desk at the end of her large office, where she has a good view of the two men who work on either side. Their manner when they step up to her desk from time to time and ask permission to speak to her is nothing less than servile. They aren't always granted their request.

For years she secretly studied and taught. But she claims she never had any problem with it, not from her family or in society. She's the mother of four children, her husband is a doctor, and as for the fact that her pupils still need protecting outside school, well yes, that's part of the transition from the old to the new times.

She has other problems. The school wall is too low, hordes of boys get up on boxes and goggle at the girls, some of whom are taught in tents because of a lack of space. There aren't enough classrooms, no playground, and the girls are hard to keep under control out of lessons. Sometimes boys even climb over the walls. They have their own psychological scars to come to terms with, as well as the girls'.

The women, the director continues, have seen terrible things. Over 50 per cent of all her pupils and teachers are traumatized. Every family has victims. This results in short attention spans, violent outbursts during lessons, paralyzing depressions and an inability to act.

Sport helps, because under physical strain they forget the psychological strain. Trips abroad would be best, to let the girls see something that they would like to pass on, something that motivates them to influence things here.

Yes, they all need a lot of patience, including the patience to be brought onto the right track educationally. 'But we have the patience, we've never expelled a pupil.'

We watch the basketball and football players training together. They are slight, not exactly tall veiled young women, but they can head a ball, stop it, pass well, and take control under a basket.

What's so moving about this activity in the hall is that it's done so seriously, and yet it's very clear that it's about having fun. The trainer controls them without being harsh, discipline is requested rather than demanded, and when screams of laughter break out, it's clear they have developed team spirit.

The surprise I feel at seeing these young women doing normal things is itself surprising. They play, chatter, laugh, scream and put their heads together. The ball is a bit flat. They all laugh. Someone fetches a pump. I admire their poster of a bare-chested muscleman on the wall. They all laugh. We let the ball go round the circle, a natural movement. Everyone laughs that this works.

'The team is the most important thing,' explains Massuda to me. 'We're friends and neighbours, but we decide as a team.'

She's one of the best at football and basketball. She'd be even better, she admits, if she didn't sometimes still mix up the two games.

Our source calls up about the interview. He's ready for a preliminary discussion. 'Drive to the Mikrorojan district. When you're there, wait for more directions.'

Nadia, Khaled and I drive out towards the edge of the city. A few trees are growing between the Russian housing blocks. Washing is hanging from the cracked balconies. If you weren't paying attention, you might confuse it with a Cold War era estate from eastern Germany.

The next call directs us through a gateway. We're asked to leave the car between the blocks of flats behind it. It's dark, and Khaled is strongly against the idea of letting us enter one of these blocks on our own. There's no other way. He'll stay in the car, keeping watch.

We get out. Two men dash into an entrance ten yards away. We can hear them climbing the stairs in the dark. We can make out two men inside the unlit van that has parked in front of the same block. Their guns lie on the seats next to them. They don't move. So we follow the other two and climb the dark stairwell to the top floor, where the door to the flat is open.

I expected an old white-haired imam. Instead a lively, bearded man in his mid-thirties is standing there, speaking English quickly, fluently and with an obvious sense of humour. His eyes are darting around and the ease with which he talks to us suggests someone who has been educated outside Afghanistan.

We can't see what's happening in the back of the flat, but he looks worried when Nadia makes a move to go into a neighbouring room to use her mobile. But there are only the obligatory dishes on the floor, surrounded by cushions. There's tea,

Nescafé and Ovaltine, which he admits to having a particular fondness for. Who would have thought that the Taliban drink Ovaltine? There are also sweets and waffles, and I can make out English titles on the bookshelves along the walls.

He looks at us with pleasure, although not cockily. The good mood in his eyes is all the more infectious for not having been expected.

'Did you learn your good English at university or abroad?' I ask.

'That's a difficult question,' he replies.

I don't see what's so difficult about the question. 'But I want to answer you honestly. I learnt it in the prisoner camp in Bagram here in Afghanistan. Is that abroad or not?'

'I think Bagram is part of the US now,' I say. From conversations with former Guantanamo prisoners I know that Bagram is in some respects harsher than the Cuban camp. There have been deaths in Bagram, and examples of psychological torture worse than those from the more famous camp.

'So does the English we're talking leave a bad taste in your mouth?'

'Of course. Other prisoners taught me it, but it's the language I was interrogated in.'

Our talk is a mixture of small talk and a probing of each other's point of view. I cautiously approach politics, and tell him how impressed I am by the population's widespread political knowledge.

'Every child is politicized,' he says proudly. 'And why? Because everyone has lost a member of their family. Who killed our uncle? Hekmatyar, who he fought against. Who's Hekmatyar? The child's told. He'll never forget.'

'And the new government?'

'There's no electricity. So the child asks who's fault it is? He's told: Ibrahim's fault. He remembers. It's Ibrahim's fault. And now take an American commander. He doesn't even know his foreign minister's name. In Bagram I once asked a US commander: What's the capital of Afghanistan? He didn't know. You're bombing Afghanistan and you don't know its capital? I asked. Orders are orders, he replied. And who's your foreign minister? It's a woman, she does a good job, he said. But he was thinking of Madeleine Albright. The only current minister he knew was Donald Rumsfeld. He's responsible for me, he said, that's the one I have to know. But the others ... It's not my job to know more.'

His points are sharp, but said in a tone that is anything but nagging, suggesting that a direct criticism of America would lower the tone. Our discussion is more like one in the West than any other I've had in this country.

At one point he puts his mobile to his ear and says a few quick sentences into it. Then he excuses himself for the interruption: 'My brother'.

I noticed, however, that no one called him. He pressed a pre-dial number and no doubt said a code word for 'Everything OK'.

I try to find out more about his life. The war comes up immediately.

'Just around the time when I came back to Afghanistan from Egypt, Massud fired one of his most powerful rockets at a square in Kabul. Around 30 people died, I'd never seen anything like it. Bodies everywhere, organs and limbs lying around, and children running between them and busily sorting out which limb went with which torso. I heard them saying, the head goes there, that leg goes over there, quick, put it in the bag. I was crying and a child came over and asked, Uncle, why are you crying? Is it your first time? Yes, my first time, I replied. Oh, the child sighed, I've seen it a lot. The first time is tough. – A child telling me that, you hear, a child!'

After a good while the conversation touches on our main concern. Everything's been decided already. The former prisoner will wait for us tomorrow morning in a house, the whereabouts of which we'll be told later. The conditions are as expected: not twisting his words, translating them well. 'And please, don't give my name. It would be dangerous for me.'

As we leave he invites us to eat with him, we decline. He gives me a biro in a pearly case. He made it himself in a prison camp in Pakistan. What a souvenir!

'Are you optimistic about Afghanistan's future?' I ask.

'It only takes seconds,' he replies, 'to destroy a house. To rebuild it takes much, much longer. Afghanistan will need a long time.'

Coming onto a roundabout Mirwais cuts in front of another car, not dangerously close – a scene that repeats itself a thousand times every day in Kabul. But the two men in the other car follow us gesturing wildly. They block the road ahead of us and walk round our car cursing us violently.

Mirwais winds the window down. The men show their IDs: police. They claim we hit and demolished their car before fleeing from the scene. Mirwais doesn't get out of the car, he speaks calmly, knowing full well that they want to be bribed off. The line of cars behind us lengthens, horns sound. The men start banging on our car, demanding that Mirwais gets out. He doesn't, appealing to them that he owes it to the woman and guest in his car to stay and protect them.

In the faces of the two men anger is rising visibly, a force that threatens to become active at any moment. Their fists are itching to hit a target. When Mirwais just drives on and the queue behind us starts moving slowly, the men react with a St. Vitus's dance. They are comic in their powerlessness. Just a banal, everyday street scene, and yet the force of the pent-up violence breaks through in a very different way than it would in Europe.

~

We watch the day's news through a snowy picture for a third time. There are long reports about the 'Paris riots'. Our Afghan friends sitting there ask what's happening. We can't tell. The pictures are overlaid with a running commentary like a sports event. Our friends' eyes show complete bafflement at this world that is violent without saying what motivates the violence.

~

The photographers on the streets of Kabul have developed their own techniques, become masters of the art of contemporary Afghan passport photography. Their colourfully decorated boxes, not much larger than shoeboxes, sit on wooden stands. The boxes come from Kabul, the lenses on the narrow front side from Russia. You sit down in front of one and are asked to look upwards, as if for a memorial. Then the photographer lifts the lens cap for an instant. After this he starts fiddling around silently and grumpily. Exactly what he's doing isn't clear. A piece of paper appears, he pushes the exposed sheet into the box's mysterious interior, sprinkles something on it, draws it through the fixer. He plucks out a small, charcoal-coloured negative, and attaches it to a little board three inches in front of the lens. The photo of the negative is then given the same treatment as the first negative. The photographer hands me a picture that looks much like any picture from the Forties.

On the side of the camera box is a little display window with photos of Massud and other bearded fighters. They seem to want to approach their own deaths, gazing far and sadly like the faces on the old porcelain plaques of Italian graves.

Our source tells us to go to the Hotel Intercontinental, where he'll phone us again. We step into the isolated world of foreign businessmen and journalists. Here on a hill outside the city limits they live in an artificial microclimate with all of their home countries' affluence. So we eat cheesecake in the bar and look at the businessmen, who all look bored. Our source phones us again, ordering us to go to the bottom of the hill. He's waiting there with a big black car. Before we have time to get out of ours and ask for new directions, he signals for us to follow him.

A short drive later down a dusty road and we're at the end of a residential area. The settlement frays here, houses are more spread out and stand lost between hilltop cemeteries. A high wall shelters a house from curious gazes.

Once we've passed the guards and been frisked, we're led up the front steps into the house. A few men sit on the veranda, obviously unhappy with our visit. Sandals in front of the door, and from an upper floor the sound of children. We wait in a cold lounge. Our source is nervous, but he greets the Guantanamo prisoner like his own son when he steps into the room.

Saif is gaunt, tall, gentle. His hand is limp when we shake it. He cowers in a chair, wrapping himself in a cloth, as he must have done on the bare floor of his camp cell. His voice is barely audible. He was only recently released from the camp. His gaze is listless. But in his features I can still make out the face I used to see on television sometimes. He was the Taliban's spokesperson, then Afghanistan's ambassador in Pakistan.

We talk quietly. Nadia translates. No, today he doesn't have the strength to talk to us, but tomorrow, tomorrow ... We believe him.

We drive through a district where many of those who have returned home live, including second generation exiles. Giant craters yawn between buildings. Most have been destroyed. Any flat still intact has been squatted. A roundabout in amongst the blocks has a flagpole and a green, reminding the locals of their Soviet rulers.

'This is where Najib was hanged, he was the Afghan president under Soviet rule,' says Mirwais, who happened to have been here at the time. 'He had applied to the UN for asylum, but in 1996 when the Taliban came, a crowd pulled him out of his house. He'd been living there almost untroubled for a while. They lynched him, stuck cigarettes in his nose and ears, and strung him up, put notes of money in his mouth, calling him a traitor.'

But Najib had tufts of hair in his fists, as was found out after his death. He must have fought back. Actually, as people later admitted, he wasn't such a bad leader for the country, given its historical circumstances.

'On the other hand,' adds Mirwais, 'as the former head of the secret service, he had many Afghans on his conscience.'

Unlike someone from our part of the world would do, Mirwais doesn't rise to a crescendo as he tells this story. He doesn't linger for a single word on the effects of the lynching. He just reports the act, without a single adjective.

~

The museum, opposite the old parliament buildings, is where Massud's troops once barricaded themselves in. Today it's in the middle of a ravaged, heavily mined area – an area where executions used to be carried out. History resonates doubly here. Each construction and square has both its own architectural, archaeological and cultural history, and a military significance. Destroyed monuments inevitably become memorials of destruction.

A policeman stands guard, a badge with an eye on it on his lapel, outside the Ethnological and Archaeological Museum that has been plundered many a time. Searching us, his hands only dare to reach down to our hips. Afterwards we pass a stone plaque which proclaims in English: 'A nation stays alive when its culture stays alive.' And it dies a little in every phrase where its culture doesn't stay alive, as this country has lived to tell.

Burdened by all the conditions imposed by different ethnic and religious groups, this culture lacks freedom, as well as points of contact to its own traditions, which are largely lost now. It also still lacks means of production and distribution systems. There's no culture here producing works and forming a public, nor will there be in the foreseeable future.

All the more impressive then the Buddhist heads at the museum's entrance, the only indications of a time when the

Hellenic and Buddhist eras fused in Afghanistan, an epoch of spiritual clarity and of a purification of the material world. For the first time outside of India the figurative representation of the Buddha was allowed. It was from here that the image of Buddha spread to China.

So the Taliban's banning and destruction of the Buddha's images appears as a sad reversal of Afghanistan's historical role. Nadia remembers a time when beautiful statues of the Buddha from the river Kunduz were carefully taken to her father, who placed them in his museum. They're lost too.

The museum's only room with exhibits makes use of counterpoint. The delicate bodies of the Buddha statues set against the roughly hewn wooden sculptures from Nuristan. They've been stood to the left and right, two ancestral lines of wall-eyed warriors from the late 18th and early 19th centuries. These life-sized men almost get lost under their helmets and weapons. Like symbolic patrons of all those who lived by the sword until recent times.

But there are women among them too. A goddess with pointed breasts rides a deer. Other women wear opulent skirts with fluted patterns over their bulging stomachs. They stare out of round eyes, their horses are decorated much as they are: their bridles and girths have geometric designs. The whole ensemble reveals how they cultivated both the erotic and the decorative. It grips you, not least because they paid little attention to physiognomy.

Nuristan, the 'Land of Light' in the northeast was considered an old pagan land, the 'Land of Unbelievers', because it was converted late. Isolated and sheltered between Pakistan and the Panjshir Valley, this region developed a unique woodworking culture.

The Nuristanis are Afghanistan's oldest inhabitants, related to the Indo-European peoples and the reason why Afghans sometimes like to trace their ethnicity to the same root as the Germans. They're blond, tall and green eyed, 'Aryans, you know', as we keep hearing. Higher up near the inaccessible former Soviet border, lives 'homo alpinus', the last survivor of a 'very old Aryan race', as research has rumoured.

I rummage through a box of international magazines at the market.

In *Spiegel* Donald Rumsfeld calls Afghanistan 'quite a success story', which 'unfortunately has been largely unnoticed'. By me too, *in situ*. We've seen American tanks emblazoned with crossed flags drive onto a roundabout swivelling their gun turrets in all directions. We've experienced provocations from this side, aggressions from that side, and witnessed American aid evaporating outside of Kabul. The war in the south doesn't abate, people are killed here daily, and it's anyone's guess what the new parliament will be able to achieve. Impossible to talk of success in the face of such a complete collapse.

'In our opinion,' Rumsfeld goes on to say, 'more countries should share in Afghanistan's success.' It's certainly true that competitive jostling has already begun, before there's even a market.

A few days ago we visited the industrial ruins of a Thirties' sugar beet factory. Each of its architectural and technical details adds to its beauty. A diaspora Afghan is now working with two businessmen from Saxony to turn this heritage building into a functioning factory again. Fields were laid out, the first test runs were carried out successfully. The plant could soon be operational, supplying a large proportion of the country's demand for sugar. It would in fact be Afghanistan's largest factory. But this uncertain success, won with the investors' own capital and personal sacrifice, breeds envy. The American administration tried to warn off the factory owners, requesting they close the plant for 'security reasons'. As it turned out, they had designs on the country's sugar supply. Everyone has their own example.

I leaf through another German magazine: 'Zsa Zsa Gabor: I'd rather cry in a Rolls-Royce than in a tram', next to 'The cultural necessity of lasting values'. Then in a Pakistani fashion magazine: 'Fair and lovely – The Miracle Maker', referring to a skin bleaching agent for Asian women, marketed by Hindustan Lever in 38 countries with the slogan 'Discover your lighter, brighter skin'. Its effects visible after six weeks of daily application. I'm told that the poorest people use these products too, because they're afraid they won't get a job or a husband otherwise.

A banker advises in a German-language magazine that 'Saving is the worst idea. Money has to be used.' Next to that an advert for the Zurich Cantonal Bank: 'Enjoy Munch's *The Scream* without being reminded of profit warnings.'

9

Cannons used to be fired from the old hilltop fortress at midday. Sometimes an enemy was tied to the muzzle of the gun.

In the valley below the Babur Gardens are being cultivated again over a wide, terraced area. Once these Gardens near the king's summer residence were the favourite place for Kabulis to go for a picnic or a day's excursion. They're named after the Afghan king and descendent of the Mongols who conquered New Delhi in 1526 and ruled as emperor over India. After the war nothing remained here but a barren field of shell-holes and split, often snapped trees.

'The trees tell us what they've experienced, too,' Mirwais says.

Behind the Gardens slums creep up the hillside. They blend into the sandy ridge as if camouflaged. Only the bright clothes on washing lines, the girls' dresses and the kites in the air add a spattering of colour to the scene. But it smells of cesspits, rubbish is rotting in the streets and sewage pours along gutters. It's as if the lid on the city has been lifted here and you can see what was under it.

The Babur Gardens lie below these settlements as a symbol of more idyllic days. The will to revive them comes from the welcome idea that both useful and beautiful things should be reconstructed. As an old song says, 'The camel needs its dates and the earth its flowers'.

Rose gardens and apple orchards can already be spied in the Gardens. Water will soon be splashing from a fountain in the semicircle of rocks. Where all the rising gravel paths converge a restorer's workshop, a summer house and a palm garden are planned. Even now this idyll is adding its own soft lines to the landscape: gardeners are praying in the flowerbeds, a couple has sat down on the lawns. A new era has begun, lovers are reclaiming their spaces.

It's astonishing enough that a royal park has been restored in this mutilated landscape, but that Kabul's zoo was maintained throughout all the years of war is straight out of a fairy tale. Who was responsible for the animals all that time? Who fed them when people barely had food? Who placed animals before people in a country where they normally aren't granted any rights? Who erected the sign that says 'Animals are God's creatures'? Who looked after them during the war?

Dreadful stories have grown up around the zoo. Stories of prisoners thrown to Marjan, a famous lion. A zookeeper is said to have fought a lion during the war, to prove his own bravery. The lion tore him to pieces. Then the zookeeper's brother killed the lion, so I'm told, by feeding him explosives.

Today the zoo is a rather rundown complex with scarcely any green – just dusty hillocks and a few over-grown enclosures where flightless birds duck into shadows, eagle owls search for night, and little signs with pictograms show who isn't present just now. One cage only contains pale bones on two wooden beds. The wolves aren't coping well with captivity and the bears pace round and round without stopping. A cartoon has been nailed to one cage. On it, animals make crazy faces at a Homo sapiens sleeping in a cage. When two women in full-length veils come past, for a second you think that you're confronted with another, different species.

But there's still a big swingboat here and a snack bar where men and women eye each other. The zoo's 60-odd species include brown and polar bears, and there's a rocky compound for monkeys where the baboons, who are separated from visitors by a brackish moat, are no better or worse behaved than anywhere else. Their movements just seem slower and more thoughtful, and their happy antics a little less zestful.

However, the little boy who comes running up to us knows otherwise. Just an hour ago a monkey managed to escape, bit a child in the leg and then hotfooted it away. The boy followed him at first, but then he lost him, he didn't stand a chance.

I ask him about Marjan the lion and his face darkens with a child's sorrow.

'Near the end he was blind, then he died. Poor Marjan, he's not alive now!' The boy tells me this as if I were Marjan's widow. He has other stories too, like the one about the boy who fell into the brown bear's enclosure. A man unwound his turban, hung it over the edge, and the boy clambered back up, back to life.

As the little boy tells us these stories his eyes are sparkling. We gradually realize that he lives in the zoo. He knows everything about it, each animal's life – they are friends he visits, and he shares their suffering. And what about his own family? His mother died giving birth to him, his father was torn apart by a mine. Every evening he walks some distance to sleep at the house of his relatives, but his real life is in the zoo.

In the large bazaar around the corner from the Ministry for Education there used to be a kiosk that sold magazines and antiques. The owner was a liberally-minded woman interested in Western culture, and harassed by the censors. So she employed a man just to ink out any exposed body parts on front pages. He closed his eyes and murmured verses from the Koran as he worked. Often people came and asked if she also had uncensored magazines. She did, and pulled out mags from under the counter that were a danger to public decency.

On the days without fresh air, there are only three types of smell in Afghanistan: the wafting haze of dust and diesel; the scent of spices, tea and roses; and last of all, putrefaction. Each smell has its own space.

Perhaps the old man experiences an acoustic equivalent as he limps down from the top floor of the office block on the market to its basement restaurant where he'll greet Nadia, his old friend's daughter. His hearing aid swings inches from his ear. Right now it's relaying the static buzz of a damaged television, then it shoots up into a piercing whistling. Now a mobile phone comes into the mix, then the muezzin's call. What reaches his ear is really just background sound. Human voices struggle to reach it. Nevertheless, his dignified gestures aren't at all affected by the insistent din in his ear.

We're planning a trip to Ghazni, a former Taliban stronghold and the place where Salema, who we met at the airport, has gone with her aunt and relatives. We'd like to surprise her there. After days of researching the road's safety, Mirwais advises us against the trip. The many gangs and highwaymen would, at best, allow us to travel non-stop and lying on the floor of the car. That would take the charm out of the trip, and whether we'd find Salema, anyway, and whether our visit would be convenient, none of that is certain. We'd like to know more about the supposed bandits, but there's no more to find out. These fighters are used to acting, not talking. So we don't go.

Turab has come from Kunduz for a cousin's engagement party. A flat tyre at the Salang Pass left him stranded in the snow for five hours. Then they hammered away until the sparks flew, improvising a solution that brought the car and all inside safely to the capital.

Now he strolls into the hotel foyer calmly, a Pine Light hanging from the corner of his mouth, the big city air surrounding him like an aura. Success! He has to spill the beans straight away:

'On the day after your women's showing 200 people came to the cinema. We haven't seen that in ages!'

Admittedly all the customers were men, and half of them had hoped to get in for free again, but at least, says Turab, the cinema is now back on the map for some people as a place to go for entertainment.

There are places that evoke memories, and there are non-places that only make people forget. We're witnessing the proliferation of such places. They're little more than storage spaces for people, as Marc Augé would say. The armies and the relief organizations active here import such non-places too: yards for offloading containers, transit areas, depots. Sometimes such non-places are transformed into places in the eyes of travellers who've spent a long time in them.

You arrive, you look around, you give the room something particular, freezing the moment. You observe people as they move, and they move other people.

'Hey mister, what's your matter?' calls out a boy in English.

'No matter.'

'What are you doing?'

'Just visiting.'

Yes, this land isn't used to visitors with an unmotivated gaze.

In the no man's land where the foreign organizations camp, Kabul has an import shop. It aims to meet the needs of soldiers of all nationalities who serve here, although in fact it caters mainly to the Americans. Besides whisky, Coke and muffins, there's always the option of buying a thermos flask printed with 'Operation Enduring Freedom'.

Beyond this area there's a ghostly gathering of different people groups. In the old industrial district here, temporary accommodation has been set up for people returning from Pakistani refugee camps. Sometimes they find space in a barrack or a tent. People try to sort out their documents and provide them with food. Outside police cars thunder by, as well as the foreign powers' tanks, jeeps and off-road vehicles, and the NGOs' minibuses. Sometimes this area must appear to new arrivals like a disaster area. Here and there a few colourful petrol pumps: modern-day shrines.

~

A former prisoner once told me about an impregnable, solitary fortress: the prison. He said it towers above an expanse dotted with bushes on the edge of the city – a place of terror.

We drive far out of the city along the road which leads to Peshawar in the end. It's unpaved, sometimes spreading out several hundred yards over the sand. The prison is visible from a distance in the middle of a giant, harvested corn field. Its high walls with castellated corner turrets enclose an area measuring almost half a square mile. The prisoner described the place well. Now I'd like to see inside it.

A few burnt-out tanks stand on the sand. A 17-year-old in uniform saunters over from the outer guardhouse, but he isn't allowed to decide whether or not we can go in. We reach the next checkpoint. There soldiers are waiting, squatting on the sand, we talk. The flags of many nations have been painted on the prison wall. Even the checkpoint itself is painted on the wall. But the commander doesn't find our visit a laughing matter. He won't even let us peek into the inner courtyard. There's something more to his harsh reaction than just a bad mood.

~

A squatting country. Even now, as it's getting cold, men still hunker by the roadside, wrapped in cloths and brown blankets. They watch the road and everyone who comes and goes, in every car. They're turned inwards and yet still taking part in events. They wouldn't do so if there wasn't so much to see when they gazed. A land of observers. Among them there's also that other one though, who rises at each car's approach and gives it a military salute. He no longer sees anything.

10

Getting a beer in 'Kabul Inn'. We enquire, knowing that people have less tolerance for drinking than for smoking dope here. The waiter nods. Of course they don't have beer. Of course he can find some. He steps to the back wall and opens a window. His hand disappears behind its curtain. After a lengthy wait, when we start to think he's forgotten all about us, he steps back over to the curtain, closes the window and picks up our cans of beer from the floor. We pay in cash. He leaves us, and in his expression we see the dealer's regret at his customers' addiction mingling with his pleasure at meeting their needs.

The next morning we drive back to the Khoshal Mina district on the edge of town. Nothing has changed since the day before. The same armed guards are at the gate, the same embarrassed, quick frisk of a body search and the same shy gesture with which we are pushed through the gate that is only open a crack. Behind it we see the same view: a pool of sandals in front of the main building's front door, a group of fighters on the ground looking at us uneasily, glimpses of flapping clothing as women flee into the house, and then to our right the same cold, unadorned room, where we wait for Saif.

He arrives without a sound, wearing the same clothes as the day before. Nothing in his face hints that he has recognized us. He sinks into the armchair as he did before, drawing his feet up underneath him and pulling his cloak tight around his gaunt body until only his head and his hands are visible. His gaze brushes gently over us, but is focused inwards: he's collecting himself for what's coming. He'll need all his strength.

A detailed interview sometimes seems a bit like an interrogation, but I want to spare him at least the language of the camp officials. Nadia interprets from Dari, and sometimes Pashto, and Saif has no objections to being interpreted by a woman, even though he is weak, naked in a way. Yet he's worried about the final translation.

'I know about these things from the old days, but also from Guantanamo. When we said something, it would be translated wrongly. What the prisoner said was twisted, for racist reasons or other motives. I have to be sure that sort of thing doesn't happen here.'

I wonder what information was supposed to be extracted in Guantanamo if not even the translations were accurate, and I promise that the utmost care will be taken.

'Good, then I agree. In God's name. You may begin.'

Together we travel back into the childhood of the Afghan village boy that he was, hungry for education, burdened by the uncertain political situation, the danger on the roads and the harshness of his life. The emerging Taliban movement met his needs in two ways: it gave him an education and security. Later it gave him a job, as the Minister for Transport, then as Afghanistan's ambassador to Pakistan.

The interview isn't easy for Saif. He struggles to speak, answers briefly and so quietly that we can barely hear him. And he repeats himself, has to start again a number of times or has to search hard for a word. He's not out to convince us, nor to accuse others. He doesn't hate – he doesn't seem to have the strength for that anymore. He reports, explains, showing astounding composure even when he talks about torture and his own tears.

A full two years before September 11th the Taliban, we hear, were negotiating Osama's extradition with the Americans. But at that point the Taliban insisted that he appear before an Afghan court, or at least an international tribunal that would include representatives of three Islamic states. The USA rejected both suggestions and insisted on their right as a superpower to act, and to judge him, on their own. The Taliban refused and Osama remained at large.

'The distance between the Americans and us was enormous. Yet our suggestions were logical, and in my opinion the Americans' suggestions weren't. They were based solely on their power. They wanted us to hand over Osama. America showed no respect. They said, "Who are the Taliban? What's Afghanistan?" The Taliban, however, didn't want to hand him over to the Americans without any evidence – until what happened on September 11th and everything got even worse.'

I know how naïve my question will sound, but I wouldn't forgive myself if I didn't ask it now. 'Did you know where Osama was hiding, even after September 11th?'

He doesn't hesitate for a second, replying as if it were just another question, 'No.'

'Where did you hear about the September 11th attacks?'

'I was at home and saw the pictures on TV.'

'Did you imagine at the time the effect that those attacks would have on Afghanistan?'

'Some people here were pleased they happened. The truth is, I cried. For two reasons. First, because a great catastrophe had happened that shouldn't have, and second, because everything that happened there was certainly going to have consequences for our country. Afghanistan would go up in flames. When September 11th happened, I condemned it on that very day, and when the Americans marched into Afghanistan I condemned that too.'

What we see in Afghanistan today is due in large measure to these events. They inform the fear, aggression, wariness and suspicion felt towards people who come from outside, whether to destroy, help or heal.

After we've been talking for several hours, in which time we move from Afghanistan to the camp in Cuba, I try to find the toilet. A little boy with muddy feet leads me to a door on the other side of the building and leaves. Through the neighbouring room's window I can see about 20 bearded warriors, squatting on the floor with their Kalashnikovs and staring hard at me. I gesture to show them that I don't want to go into their room, just the toilet next door. No reaction. So I open the loo door, undo my belt, and – the knocking on the door isn't a knocking. It's a thundering, and it shakes the whole door. My heart beating wildly, I pull up my trousers, unbolt the door and open it an inch, ready for anything. A full-bearded warrior stands at the door. Expressionless, he stretches out his arm, holding a roll of toilet paper.

Saif tells us about his route through the camps, his years in Guantanamo and their devastating effect on his mental and physical health. It shakes us. Hours later we arrive in the present.

'Are you able to work again now?'

'No. I've forgotten everything I knew. For example, I used to work at a computer. Now I can't even type. Everything's gone from my memory. I have to re-learn it all. The same with everything else. These past four years I didn't see a book, hold a pen, learn anything, or hear or read a thing. I was completely cut off, my memory and head don't work well because I had nothing to do but think. It's obvious: anyone who spends all day, all year, all his life thinking, will go mad. It was agony.'

'Do you enjoy reading now?'

'I can't do it, it doesn't work. I bought a lot of books, there they are – in the other room. I haven't read a single book yet. I manage to stick at it for ten minutes, that's my limit.'

'Can you listen to music?'

'I don't want to.'

'Is nature something you enjoy?'

'I haven't been outside yet. People tell me that I have to take care because of the security situation. I stay home, try to read, and have visitors that I talk to. I wanted to write a book, but I couldn't.'

'How do you explain to yourself the fact that you didn't break?'

'The Americans asked me that too. How come you don't go crazy? If we were here for just one month we'd go crazy. They really said that. We only had the Koran, nothing else.'

After this answer, his strength is exhausted. He asks if he can stop and leave. His first month of freedom is coming to an end, a freedom that doesn't yet deserve that name.

~

A motorbike, a horse-drawn cart, sometimes a herd appear in

the distance from between the dunes – which is also to say, from between the villages, which nestle on the far side of the hills, invisible from the road. Sometimes funeral processions come over the hills, or a group of mourners stands in a forest of flags that even from a distance we recognize as a cemetery. Once only ten people had gathered there. Mirwais explains laconically, 'They are burying a child. Everybody comes for the old. Children are too young to have known many people.'

11

Sometimes you enter an unreal landscape, and sometimes one unreality leads into another like a suite of interconnected rooms. There's a brown, barren hill beyond the city, a wound in the earth that's just recently scabbed over. An eerie atmosphere hangs over it. Here the mujaheddin captured enormous amounts of weaponry and the Taliban had their arsenal. The Americans bombed the hill incessantly, it burnt day and night. At the foot of the hill there was once a training ground.

Today part of the plain has been reclaimed for something surprising: a golf course. For the rich exiles returning home, for the offspring of families who profited from the wars, for foreign relief workers? Two groups are now playing golf on this field that used to be heavily mined. Even if rubbish is collecting under the embankment, the greens are bumpy, and the grass is yellow, the game is certainly recognizable as golf.

And that's just for starters. The dam that rises over the course holds a reservoir of milky, opalescent green water for the city's millions. Nadia tells us of a stocky, strident-voiced development worker from Germany, a real livewire, who trained policemen in lifeguard skills at this artificial lake. You can imagine her standing there with her balled fists on her hips, as the forces of law and order swim for their lives.

The view from the dam takes in a whole panorama of today's Afghanistan – from the steep rocky mountainsides down to the wheezing city's smog; from the legacy left by bombs and shells, across farmers' orchards and the strange golf course, to the welcoming banks of the reservoir where rowing boats bob on the low water; from the dead ground to the spit of land where the first Western-influenced tourist café has sprung up along with its own boat hire, greenhouses and pagodas for holiday-makers.

They call it a club. It probably only exists because homesickness inclines people, particularly among the relief agencies, towards such a place. After everything we've experienced, it's hard to believe what we see as we step through wild silk curtains onto the veranda. We find a good 120 shiny cantilevered leather chairs from the Forties arranged around little tables that are spread out on a number of terraces. Carpets, kilims, textiles from Nuristan, mirrors, inlaid work in stone and in ceramic tiles, and a bar well stocked with spirits all add to the scene.

Its use of space is subtle, brought about with indirect, intimate lighting. Tent-like hangings provide an inviting privacy for groups, there is a 'Pool Site', and soon you will be able to hire horses here too. Is the country healing, here in its nouveau riche culture?

Khaled, in any case, is astonished. Then he blurts out, 'Oh, peace is wonderful!'

After our excursions into Afghanistan's archaic history, here is its newest location. Its sign welcomes visitors and the future with the English words 'No Guns Allowed!'

The old rural houses that haven't been destroyed look like objects uncovered in an archaeological excavation, the faces we see there are like terracotta antiquities.

And then near the road behind Paghman children appear from the nomads' tent camp. They're wearing woolly jumpers (one with 'Yes, Mum' written on it), and their traditional gold-embroidered waistcoats over the jumpers. Shivering, they cling to their freezing animals. When a thunder storm follows a few cold nights they all huddle closer together for a warmth that only comes from each other.

Every morning the nomad children walk to a nearby school for a few hours' teaching. Then some of them work for the road builders. Even the very old nomads are occupied, gathering fruit and walnuts, or dried dung to burn as fuel. The toothless faces of these old men and women are like pencil drawings, composed only of lines. As soon as they enter their tents they disappear under blankets. Sacks of corn lie around, and things to use as fuel. Tin dishes hang from the ridge of the tent. After years of use each object has lost its lustre, and tells a story. Finally, an old man takes a blanket and covers the calves.

A little further and we're already among the martyrs' graves. Sometimes their green pennants are made of precious silk. Threadbare, they flutter in the wind, soaked tatters that will stand up to the weather for a time.

And so the settlements give way to cemeteries, and the cemeteries to the nomads' camps, and up at the top of the hill, where the Star House once welcomed the king for his holidays, the mercenary commander Sayaf lives in an isolated mansion, guarded on all sides and intimidating to whoever lives in its shadow. A warlord not long ago, he has become a member of parliament. His people in this area have his picture in their living rooms – some out of gratitude, others out of fear. 'Where is my burial cloth, on which to record my deeds?' as Atiq Rahimi wrote.

Khaled, a lab technician by profession, used to walk in this region from one village of nomads to the next in order to vaccinate the poorest. Often they didn't want to let him go, so great was their hospitality.

Children stand with clasped hands at the entrance to their village and stare. If you hold their gaze they start laughing at their own curiosity.

~

A tiny well-fortified village completely encircled by a wall. Over to one side a donkey spews red mush. At first we are denied entry – out of fear, defensive instinct or shame? – but then we are let in after all.

The person who leads us inside, risking his neighbours' opposition, is a 21-year-old soldier on home leave. Fighting still occurs in the southern province of Sabul where he serves. American soldiers 'cleanse' settlements, as is said here too, and the boy is among those who form the Afghan vanguard.

He leads us into a small house. The cold living room is painted yellow and only sparsely decorated with red blankets and carpets. As we sit, drinking tea and eating nuts, his story slowly opens a window onto this war in the south that we around the world hear about, but have very little real notion of, and that he can't tell his mother about, as he adds quietly. Otherwise she wouldn't let him leave again. It's very peaceful where I am, he always says, very peaceful.

In fact he was caught in a Taliban ambush only last week. Two fellow soldiers didn't survive. Shortly before that two cars were hit by mines and an American died too. A month ago in Shepherd's Valley twelve Afghans lost their lives, as well as three US soldiers. He tells us this without any expression on his face, merely documenting events. This makes it all the more horrific.

'The people in Sabul are wild, even the children wear turbans. Even Arabs and Pakistanis are fighting there. Only the women aren't. The Americans took revenge for the death of their soldiers and killed the village commander. That started a gun fight in which the commander's daughter was wounded too. Then we captured the next commander. He was dragged off, where to – we don't know. We aren't told anything. The Americans just drag off prisoners. None of them has been seen again.'

'Who goes first into the villages where you're fighting?'

'We always do. We go in first. They stay on the hill and wait until we've searched everywhere.'

He says this without an accusatory tone, but with scorn.

'They're afraid.'

'And what if you refused to obey the order?'

'We did once. We'd been marching all day and wanted to sleep in the desert. But the Americans ordered us not to. We were so tired that we almost got into a fist fight about it. Then we got our way. It wouldn't have been good for the Taliban to see us like that.'

'Are there friendships between the Afghan and American soldiers?'

'At war there can be no friendship with the USA.' A pause.

'And privately?'

'Nor privately.'

'When are you called up? What training are you given?'

'Some of our Uzbeks were called up at 15. They get three months' training, learn how to storm a yard, to enter a house and how to use violence if someone resists. They even learn a little bit of first aid.'

'15-year-olds?'

'Yes.'

'What are your rations?'

'Bread made from wheat flour, yoghurt that still moves, potato goulash.'

'Are your nerves up to the war?'

He smiles shyly with each answer he gives, looking intently at us out of his big dark eyes, as if he has to promote himself with his words. But now he passes his long, fine-fingered hand briefly over his eyes. 'Nothing scares me any more. I've seen too much already.'

'Have you ever felt for your enemies?'

'Yes, they have families too, have mothers and fathers. They're just being used too. They're forced to fight and don't have any choice.'

Two others chip in, 'That's right, so right!'

'And are there good commanders?'

'No. If you ask me: no. They build themselves houses made of gold.'

He has enlisted for four years, in return for starvation wages. Yes, he did it for the money, how else should he survive? He's cannon fodder, he knows it, and uses a similar expression himself. 'If we had peace, I'd do any job.'

'Which in particular?'

'Any job that helped peace,' he says.

'Did you vote?'

'Of course I voted. I've seen so many dead and wounded, I have to have some hope.'

'And do you have hope in the new government?'

'Yes,' he smiles his shy smile. 'Why not?'

But it sounds fatalistic, although he doesn't intend it to.

Someone is kicking up a fuss outside. Not everyone is happy with our visit. Suddenly the young soldier shows himself as man of the house. 'Tell them to be quiet. This is my house, and I'm in charge here.'

He really is the head of the household, the eldest of eight sisters and ten brothers.

'They're all still alive,' he says smiling. It's clear that he's played a part in this and is proud of it, with good reason. I look around: an unadorned room, rather smoky, a bare hill through the front door, mud houses, winter closing in. This is the place a soldier longs for. He'll dream of this place, starting tomorrow, when he leaves the village again to fight in the south for something that isn't his, that he doesn't believe in, that will cost other people their lives at his hand, and maybe cost him his own too.

~

Travelling back along the mud track we pass the nomads' camp again. Suddenly someone materialises in the road: a trouserless eight-year-old with a large stone in his hand is blocking our way. The expression in his eyes is wild, his pose is devil-may-care, his gaze can't be met with any words. He is just standing there, threatening the car with his raised throwing arm, muttering and panting. In his breathless rage and heroism he is so out of control and helpless that we can barely look at him. He might explode any minute, go off the rails, free himself from himself. Perhaps he's one of the traumatised children that you meet all around here, or perhaps he was born disturbed. In any case, the expression he adopts is of the powerless soldier who only has stones to fight his enemy with.

Mirwais grabs a fistful of nuts and raisins from our provisions and cautiously approaches the little boy. He gently extricates the stone from the threatening fist and pours the nuts in. But the boy is unable to hold them. He only manages to gobble up a few from his flat hand. The rest of them land in the dust. No one says a word.

Not much further on we pass a little girl with a look of intense love in her eyes. She's squeezing a rooster so tightly in her arms that his eyes are popping out of his head and he's squawking terribly. Some things can only be explained by the war.

The go-between calls up, invites us to a meal. I decline, having been invited to an engagement party that evening. He says I should cancel. I don't.

Kabul is experiencing a marriage boom. It has come since music has been allowed at weddings. Houses are often much too small for the celebrations. If you peer through the big windows of the city's wedding halls you will see men dancing with other men, and women with other women. Even these modern Las Vegas-style temples can't alter the tradition of separating the sexes during weddings.

The engagement in the house of one of Nadia's distant relatives is a liberal affair. Magnificently clothed and scented

Afghan women (how much we miss seeing the women's faces!) step into the vestibule of the host's house before disappearing into the women's area, the basement. The men and women only meet briefly in the reception room and in the courtyard where food is being cooked and grilled in giant pots, basins and pans. Yet they almost ignore each other.

While the women go downstairs to a hall from which smoke and music soon rise, the men make their way to a side lounge, where the 30 of them sit in a circle on the floor and pass the time in silence. The old prophets with their white beards and turbans have wrapped themselves in cloths and squat motionlessly. Turab fidgets, swaps places often, makes faces and – troublemaker that he is – whispers to me, 'You are the guest, just go down to the women in the cellar!'

Mirwais is the messenger between the men's and women's areas. 'The engaged couple are sitting on thrones in the hall now.'

And I meet two young emigrants who have returned home from the USA and perhaps do, perhaps don't, want to stay. Like the fiancé, they fall between countries, generations, languages, ethnic groups and eras. They take part greedily in American culture, scarcely knowing how to counter it with their own culture, yet they move confidently and sincerely among the strange traditions and rituals.

Through Mirwais, Nadia asks me to come outside. She's been swept up in the party atmosphere, has danced and is beaming. Her joy is infectious. A camera team disappears into the basement, the music has become more unbridled. We even hear screaming, and again everything that makes up Afghanistan's female world is out of my sight. So let's stay and wait for the men's area to liven up.

Entering the men's lounge, the old men greet me with a nod of their heads. One and a half hours of sitting together has brought us closer. Then in no time the tablecloth is rolled out on the floor and dishes are passed along a well organised line of people: bread, two kinds of rice, ragout, kebabs, two colours of jelly. We begin the ritual meal, eat in silence, and half an hour later it's as if the meal had never existed. All the plates have been cleared away, the old men are sitting down again, silent as ever, while the women in the cellar are a noisy threat to morality. Bollywood music, instruments being played live, even chirping singing.

When I leave I'm allowed to go upstairs to the couple's chamber, which is more of a giant pink chocolate box full of presents, as sweet as it is pompous. The bride-to-be is standing there in a matching pink, as pretty as an exhibit, almost translucent in her happiness and worry. Beside her stands her fiancé, a refugee who has returned from Pakistan, dignified but brawny, and perhaps for that reason too clumsy to play an entirely elegant part in the ceremony.

Going back through the courtyard after nightfall, I see they're still cooking.

'We always put the coals first under the pots and then later on their lids, so that they stay hot,' Mirwais explains as conspiratorially as if he were revealing the secret recipe for a happy marriage.

~

The country is not bound by old limits, Kabul is expanding uncontrollably, the post-war situation is delicate. This is the situation in which the country is forming its constitution. Eight wise people are working on it, including two women.

I ask one of them, a woman who is highly educated in legal matters, which specifically female issues she managed to get into the constitution.

'It wasn't difficult,' she replies, 'to have a clause added to the constitution that says: all people are equal before the law. What was difficult was making explicit that women are meant by that too. The men always said that it was clear, and we replied: well, if it's clear, then it should be stated expressly. We won through.'

They negotiated for a year, specifying rights for widows and children. They studied the old constitution and also some European constitutional documents, as well as those from Islamic countries. American advisors offered their services too. After six months the constitutional commission consulted around 30 people from all the different provinces. They struggled to bring the constitution into line with the different tribes' and ethnic groups' traditions. Of course it resulted in a compromise, but one that can hold.

'I'm happy with it,' she said. 'But please don't mention me by name.'

Overnight the winter has arrived, crisp and windless. We drive to one of the returnee camps where washing hangs between the wrecks of Russian tanks and the ruins of abandoned houses. So this is where those people who follow the politicians' promises and return from Pakistan end up. The buildings often have no roof, their outside walls are damaged and offer almost no protection from the cold. The façades are full of little nooks. They look like slits to shoot out of, but they provide a flow of fresh air. For decades wine pressing has been banned according to the constitution. At harvest time the grapes are hung in the rooms to dry and become raisins. An old man gives me a handful. His fist has warmed them.

'We fought for a humane life for 20 years, and where did it get us? To these mountains.'

Just a few miles further on, a refugee camp sits on the spur of a gently rising mountain. When the snows melt, perhaps the river will carry water for the first time in seven years. But then there might be avalanches of mud that pick up mines or bury whole families, as they have in the past. Here in the mountains relief organizations ensure that water is provided. Men, women and children leave over the snowy hills with water in three sizes of canister, heading for a rocky wall, in which their huts sit like bird boxes.

They head for the distant villages too. Children old before their time, green-eyed witches, small women in ragged post-war coats and headscarves, one wearing a silk dress and wellies, ancient shrunken people with their features carved deep into their faces. Sometimes they each have only a block of ice in their canister after their journey, sometimes only a single flat bread that they clutch to their chest.

The refugees are sent from Iran and Pakistan into a void, because it's said to be peaceful now. President Karzai appeals to people to return. They do, and fetch up almost without shelter on mountain slopes, to die of hunger or freeze to death. On arriving they find ruins.

A woman fled to the Peshawar refugee camp 22 years ago when her house was completely destroyed in heavy bombing. Her name is Sebogol, 'beautiful flower'. Her husband fell in their homeland. Recently she dared to return to the edge of Kabul, found the ruins of her house and made it habitable. She has rarely been into the city itself. It's too dangerous there. Women prefer to let their husbands do the shopping.

Some from the Peshawar camp found a precarious home in the ruins of the university, with 400 other families. They were driven out, fled into the mountains, and were moved on again. The eldest refugee went to President Karzai and obtained a reprieve: the camp on the slope can stay, the 1,200 households will be tolerated, although their prospects aren't rosy.

'We will live here as long as we live,' he says. 'We don't have any electricity, any shelter, any water. What's the good of politics? I'm an old man and have spent my whole life fighting, and where have I ended up? Here!'

From his hillside position he surveys the resting places of the dead.

Afghanistan is in the grip of its coldest winter for twenty years. It's minus 20 degrees. Even in Kabul, where some people have at least generators, that's bitterly cold. While in the refugee camps children meet us with flip-flops on their otherwise naked feet.

'What's up?' a nine-year-old calls out in English, strutting up like a used car salesman.

He arrived from Peshawar two years ago and lives with eight others in a room without electricity. 'Very bad,' he describes the situation, acting cool with his hand in his jacket, tucked under his armpit. I understand the pose later: fighters would keep a hand on their shoulder holster, and the children are copying this.

The camp chief invites us into his house for tea, coconut sweets and piped biscuits. They all fought, but in 'self-defence', they stress. They didn't chose politics, but politics chose that the people of Afghanistan would be crushed between other peoples' interests. Everything else was a result of that. The oldest man, who is also the judge, is wearing a military coat.

'Even if there is a Russian embassy in Kabul,' he says, 'it's the Russians who brought chaos. We'll always hate them.'

'And what did you think when the US bombed Kabul?'

'You're asking questions for a president to answer. I'm just a homeless person,' he answers with a judge's reserve.

The snowy landscape around us is gouged by deep chasms. Frost has cracked the mud bricks of the houses. Parents here were wary of NGOs at first, but their opposition dissipated when CARE organized lessons in these remoter areas, setting about supplying both food and sustainable education. Not even the fact that all 24 schools give lessons for boys and for girls causes problems any longer.

The girls tell their stories. In every one there are dead people. But nowadays the way to school is short and safe, sisters and parents help them with their homework, and the coming of spring is always beautiful in these mountains.

One of the fathers made his own house available for the girls' classes.

'It's better today,' they chorus.

'Why?'

'Because we aren't being killed. Because we're allowed to be Muslims. Because we want to be doctors, teachers and engineers.'

It's natural. They go to the doctor's, the teacher visits them, and they're all hoping for engineers. Only one of the girls doesn't want her photo taken – so that her parents don't see her like this.

In the meantime a fighter has stood up on a cart outside – a real fighter, but an idiot too. He's gap-toothed and in great spirits. His voice rings out over the small square. 'We don't need a government that doesn't care! We've rebuilt everything here ourselves. We're tired of fighting, but if nothing changes we'll take up arms again.'

He shakes his crooked stick over people's laughing heads. 'Be quiet, this is the truth!'

Everyone laughs. 'He's right, he's right!'

His voice drowns out everyone else as he climbs higher up the cart, swinging his sceptre. 'Salaam alaikum, Charlie Charlie.'

He thinks the last words are German. Then he hisses, 'Give me work. I can do anything. Whatever you want, I'll be up to it.'

Everyone laughs.

Inside the children are having a lesson about mines. As the teacher's pointer passes from one object to the next, they name all the deadly weapons.

'And which of you have already seen a real mine?'

Many hands shoot up. Children's faces beam, proud that they have too. Out on the fields white stones mark where mines have been cleared, red stones mark the areas that are still mined. Now the snow has turned everything white.

'And how did you protect yourselves?'

'We dug bunkers with our hands,' one girl says.

An orchard has been planted in the school's inner yard. Its harvest will supplement the teachers' meagre pay.

'When the Taliban ruled, I learnt secretly,' says the female teacher. 'In my head and my heart. Now I can learn openly. It's an honour for me.'

Even she, a modern Afghan woman, sometimes chooses to wear the burka outside of work.

Standing on the school's roof you can sense the progress in this region. The fields on the slopes are terraced. You can hear roosters, the distant hammering of workers and the farmers' calls. At this hour of the morning spring is in the air, and it's hard to believe that one of the main lines of battle ran through here for a long time. Sometimes a single white kite rises over the snowy landscape. As soon as you see it you think: thank God, someone's playing.

On the way to the airport we see a horse pulling a cart. It's carrying a string of fish next to a string of sparrows. The shimmer of the fish scales has tarnished, and the sparrows' wings are frayed. Both the fish and sparrows will be smoked in the city smog. Then a policeman halts the cart and starts to push it into a side street himself. 'Out of the way! President Karzai is about to come by with his cavalcade!'

The seller is amazed. Can't the president bear the sight of a cart?

What do we hold onto when we leave? To two carrier bags full of almonds from Kunduz that Turab gives us just before we go, a child's waistcoat from Central Afghanistan, a lapis lazuli box, and a talisman against the evil eye. Turab hurries his goodbyes, rubbing his sunken, unshaved cheeks against mine twice. Mirwais gazes at the floor, holding his tasbeeh tight in his left hand. We kiss three times, our hands grasp each other's upper arms a little too long, then we let go.

'I'll miss you.'

He nods. Then there's the madness of family scenes, people sobbing and not being able to let go, the commanding voices at security checks, the customs officials' imperious gestures, the porters' shouts and the blind attempts of those in charge to conduct it all.

'Senda bashi!' Mirwais said. 'Be alive!' Seeing Afghanistan lying below me, that's just what I think.

Acknowledgements

I have much to thank Nadia Karim for. No words of thanks are enough. Here I thank her for her tireless care and support, and her courageous willingness to let me see her country through her eyes. Many thanks to her for everything she brought to this book, and to her cousins Mirwais-jan and Turab-jan, who today mean so much to me.

Thanks to Nadja Malak and Wolfgang Jamann from CARE International for accompanying me so helpfully on my first trip to Afghanistan.

Thanks also to Anette Henke, on whose support and organisational skill I have been able to rely for so long, and to my English publisher Barbara Schwepcke and my translator Stefan Tobler.

Donations:
CARE International UK
www.careinternational.org.uk